POETIC VOYAGES
WESTERN KENT

Edited by Simon Harwin

First published in Great Britain in 2002 by
YOUNG WRITERS
Remus House,
Coltsfoot Drive,
Peterborough, PE2 9JX
Telephone (01733) 890066

HB ISBN 0 75433 408 2
SB ISBN 0 75433 409 0

FOREWORD

Young Writers was established in 1991 with the aim to promote creative writing in children, to make reading and writing poetry fun.

This year once again, proved to be a tremendous success with over 88,000 entries received nationwide.

The Poetic Voyages competition has shown us the high standard of work and effort that children are capable of today. It is a reflection of the teaching skills in schools, the enthusiasm and creativity they have injected into their pupils shines clearly within this anthology.

The task of selecting poems was therefore a difficult one but nevertheless, an enjoyable experience. We hope you are as pleased with the final selection in *Poetic Voyages Western Kent* as we are.

CONTENTS

Poverest Primary School

Thomas Whelan	76
Megan-Rose Lightwing	76
Michael McGuire	77
Grace Gaywood	78
Steven Cresswell	78
Lauren Sweetlove	79
Sianna Louise Grover	79
Samuel Hanson	80
Cathy Alcoran	80
Jade Young	81

Raglan Primary School

Rosie Yates	82
Kate Giannini	83

Rangefield Primary School

Beverley Agyeman	83
Jamie Muller	84
Robert Allen	84
Natasha Wilkinson	85
Liam Dorta-Martin	85
Thomas Allen	86
Anders Wickham	87
Stacey Rogers	87
Amy Hayden	88
Lucy Bick	88
Brett Dowling-Jones	89
Taylor Wallace	89
Kelly Foxcroft	90
Brogan Green	90
Sophie Savage	91
Charlotte Wingfield	91
Jennifer Forde	92
Bonita Brindle	92
Micheala Virgo	93
Anusha Badal	93
Kayla Patricia Dawkins	94
Lucy Toomey	94

Samantha Gleeson	95
Michael Dorey	96
Aisha Derbel	96
Thomas Hogg	97
Bethany Rooks	97
Daniel Reeves	98
Aylin Unlu	98
Leia Thomas	99
Cilem Karabeyaz	100

Seal CE Primary School

Rebecca Collins	100
Martin Roff	100
Amanda McGinniss	101
Stephanie Coppins	101
Anthony Stewart	101
Lee Roberts	102
Chloe Checkley	102
Scott Nowers	103
Jade King	103
Lily Rose	104
Gemma Scott	104
Heidi Jessop	104
Tamanna Miah	105
Sophie Primett	105
Tanya Waghorn	106
Samuel Kettle	106
Zoe Dunmill	107
Jacob Lowe	107
Adam Orme	108

Sevenoaks Prep School

Jonathan Stowell	108
Antony Grant	109
Josh Perry	110
Sam Hull	110
Sam Cox	111
Oliver Parrett	112

The Poems

SMUGGLERS

A cave is on a cliff
It is guarded by a smuggler called Tiff.
A cave is a smuggler's hideout,
It is next to a pond with a lot of trout.

I am around, I'll give you some tea.
I don't want you to see.
Dare you to walk into a cave,
You might end up as a slave.

There's a smuggler with a big belly,
He is a bit smelly.
I'll give you tea,
From across the sea.
Don't look there's a spy
Turn around as they go by.

Turn around I'll give you some tea.
I don't want you to see.
Dare you to walk into a cave
You might end up as a slave.

Lewis Ruffle (10)
Broadwater Down Primary School

WISH

I've always wished to see London
And to go to Egypt.
I wish I could live forever
And be on Friends.
I wish I was a teacher reading a story
And I could ride on roller skates.

Amanda Mastars (8)
Broadwater Down Primary School

MY UNCLE JIM AND AUNTIE LYN

I have an auntie called Lyn,
She is funny but a little bit dim.
When we're out shopping,
She starts hopping and popping.
Isn't she a strange Auntie Lyn?

When we get home I used the phone,
To ring my uncle Jim.
He comes over from Dover,
And my auntie goes back to the loony bin
And I start to moan because I should have known.

When he comes over he always has his Clover,
And he acts like he has been crowned
And I start to frown.
Sometimes I think he is a clown.
Oh I wish I'd never picked up the phone.

Kimberley Rattray (12)
Broadwater Down Primary School

SCARY ALIENS

I know an alien ten foot tall
Gave me a fright and sent me to school.
I know an alien who had a hairy belly
Sent me to bed and scared off my head.
I know an alien who turned on my light
And said goodnight,
Shut the door
And the rain started to pour.
I know an alien who pushed my mum
Scared me to death and pushed me out the door
I opened my eyes and fell on the floor.

Sinead Elliott (7)
Broadwater Down Primary School

CHRISTMAS DAY

It was waking up at 6 am and creeping downstairs to have a look.
It was going into my brother's room to tell him we had lots of presents.
It was having chocolatines for breakfast.
It was eating chocolate with pleasure.
It was opening my presents with excitement.
It was having Great Nanna round for Christmas.
It was eating Christmas lunch with delight.
It was playing with my magic set.
It was playing with my brother on his new computer disc.
It was playing table football with joy.
It was opening paint pots with glowing colours.
It was making my Lego model.
It was going to bed excitedly, ready for the next day.

Robert Harris (8)
Broadwater Down Primary School

MEMORIES OF HASTINGS

The sight of seagulls in the sky flying high,
The boats sitting on the pebbles, the big buildings standing tall.

The taste of fresh orange juice and chips melting in your mouth,
The vinegar on your chips.

The smell of crabs and fish and the salty sea,
Also the wet and damp caves.

The feel of drops of rain falling on you,
The breezy wind.

The sounds of waves splashing,
The rough voice of hairy Jack, people laughing
And screaming.

Emel Karagoz (10)
Broadwater Down Primary School

SMUGGLERS

If you wake at dark
And see the dark,
If you see the smugglers
Smuggling,
Don't go muttering.

If you hear a horse's feet,
Trotting in the street
And if you see the gin,
Don't go throwing it in the bin.

If you see a spy,
Go and tell a lie,
If you see their goods,
They are hidden in their hoods.

If you hear a horse's feet,
Trotting in the street
And if you see the gin
Don't go throwing it in the bin.

Courtney Punyer (9)
Broadwater Down Primary School

POSTMAN TOM

Postman Tom, Postman Tom,
Postman Tom ran over a bomb,
Postman Tom was crying,
As he was slowly dying,
He'd got blood all over his favourite hat.

Postman Tom, Postman Tom,
Postman Tom had survived from that bomb,
He turned on his computer,
Typed in 'Please Miss Hooter,
If you don't save me I will die.'

Postman Tom, Postman Tom,
Postman Tom, was now scared of bombs,
That were in the London museum,
Owned by Mr Leom,
He got so scared, he wet his pants.

Adam Waring (10)
Broadwater Down Primary School

MEMORIES OF HASTINGS

Looking at the chips and burgers,
Looking at the smelly boats,
Looking at the teachers talking,
Looking at the Smuggles show.

Tasting the chips with ketchup,
Tasting the orange squash,
Tasting the burger with ketchup,
Tasting the vinegar on my chips.

Smelling the smelly boats,
Smelling the salty water,
Smelling the food of my dinner,
Smelling the vinegar on my chips.

Touching the rough stones,
Touching the boat in the museum,
Touching the caves walls,
Touching the burger in a roll.

Listening to the seagulls,
Listening to the hairy Jack,
Listening to the crying,
Listening to the sound of eating.

Kayleigh Greagsby (8)
Broadwater Down Primary School

MEMORIES OF HASTINGS

The sight of seagulls swooping down,
The sight of the building in the old town.

The taste of the vinegar on the chips,
The taste of orange, in little sips.

The smell of the fish in the sea,
In the cafe Mrs Ellis makes a cup of tea.

The feel of rain on my hair,
In the cave, I thought there was a bear.

The sound of the pebbles washing away,
In the fisherman's museum, we didn't have to pay.

Daniel Ellis (8)
Broadwater Down Primary School

MEMORIES OF HASTINGS

The sight of soft sand,
In your cosy little hand.

The sound of seagulls swooping down,
It is so smelly in that old, old town.

The taste of frying chips,
Don't eat them or they'll hurt your lips.

The smell of fish is great.
To catch them you need bait.

The feel of cold wind in your face,
It follows you in every place.

Robert Chantler (8)
Broadwater Down Primary School

BUSY TOWN

People carrying sticks,
Some five foot, some six,
Buildings to your right
A good view of the site.
Buckets lying on the floor,
One building is missing a door.
Birds in the sky,
If I saw this place, I would sigh.
There is a dog running through the river
If I was him, I would get fed up and shiver.

On the river there is a boat
Nine out of ten are wearing a coat,
People talking, quite a few walking along
In my picture.

Charlie Tampsett (8)
Broadwater Down Primary School

MEMORIES

The sight of seagulls coming down,
The sight of buildings in the old town,
The taste of fried chips,
The taste of burgers that burn my lips,
The smell of the crab's legs,
The smell of smugglers' peg legs,
The smell of the slimy walls,
The feel of the smooth pebbles,
The sound of seagulls squeaking,
The sound of cars scrunching.

Daniel Tinham (9)
Broadwater Down Primary School

LATE

Went in the kitchen,
Tap cried 'Turn me on'
'Can't' I said, 'Late.'

Went into the bathroom
Flannel wept 'Dry me'
'Can't' I said, 'Late.'

Went outside,
Cat whined, 'Feed me'
'Can't' I said, 'Late.'

Went in the garden
Window whispered 'Open me'
'Can't' I said, 'Late.'

Went to the shed
Frisbee shouted 'Throw me'
'Can't' I said, 'Late.'

Went indoors,
Mum screams 'Eat your tea'
'Can't' I said, 'Late.'

Zara Lucas (10)
Broadwater Down Primary School

ONE EVENING

One evening my mum kissed the light
And turned off me.
Closed the floor
And walked on the door.
Ate the stairs
And walked down the pears.

Kierran Smallwood (8)
Broadwater Down Primary School

THERE WAS . . .

There was an old man from Bristol,
Who had a loaded pistol,
He shot a fat hen
And a boy called Ben,
That nasty man from Bristol.

There was a girl called Claire,
Whose head was very bare,
She wore a hat,
Fancy that,
The poor old girl named Claire.

There was a boy called Joe,
Who ate a lot of dough,
He saw a dog,
Sat on a frog,
That silly old boy called Joe.

There was a girl called Hannah,
Who had a heavy hammer,
She broke her leg,
So she went to bed,
That poor old girl called Hannah.

Chloe Barrow (11)
Broadwater Down Primary School

VERY FAT MAN

There was a very fat man,
Who ate a lot of spam,
He got heavy and round
And fell through the ground
And now he will only eat ham.

Matthew Gillan (10)
Broadwater Down Primary School

I Met An Lion

I met a lion
That was crying.
I met a hawk,
That couldn't talk.
I met a snail,
Which was old and frail.
I met a cow,
Who knew how to bow.
I met a worm,
That made me squirm.
I met a man,
That had a fan.
I met a snake,
That looked like a rake.
I met a bear,
That sat on a chair.
I met a cat,
That looked like a mat.
I met a pig,
That wore a wig.
I thought to myself,
I'll run away with stealth.

William Barnard (10)
Broadwater Down Primary School

Tounge Twisters

Jake is a snake
A slithering, snake,
A slimy, slithering snake,
A slithering, slimy snake,
A strong, slithering, slimy,
Snake.

Ryan is a rhino
A rough rhino,
A running, rough, rhino,
A red, ripe, running, rough, rhino.

Ryan Bunce (8)
Broadwater Down Primary School

I MET A WOLF

I met a wolf,
Who ate a dwarf.

I met a dragon,
With a double Magnum.

I met a tiger,
Who was a hiker.

I saw a lion,
With an iron.

I met a bird,
Who was a nerd.

I met a worm,
That had a germ.

I met a monkey,
Who was very funky.

I met a goat,
That . . . in a moat.

I met a man with a gun
Who had a bullet in his thumb.
I whacked him on the head
And then he went all red.

Chris Stevens (10)
Broadwater Down Primary School

AWESOME SEASONS

W rap up warm,
I   cy lakes,
N ights are dark,
T   rees are bare,
E choing nights,
R oaring fires.

S inging birds,
P arks are busy,
R oses are blossoming,
I   ndigo sky,
N ew life,
G rowing leaves.

S un shines bright,
U nbearable heat,
M unching salad,
M elting Mars bars,
E ating ice lollies,
R esting on the beach.

A nimals hiding,
U nusual sounds,
T urning leaves,
U mbrellas are essential
M isty mornings,
N ights are long.

Mark Hemsley (10)
Broadwater Down Primary School

THE RIVER

The
  Rivers
    Wave
      A
        Gentle
       Hand,
     Swirling,
      One way,
        Swishing
          That way
       Having
    Fun
    All
  Day
Long.

Jennifer Mercer (10)
Broadwater Down Primary School

FAIRIES MAGIC

Fairies are colourful,
Fairies are beautiful,
Fairies are magical,
Fairies are powerful,
Fairies are kind,
Fairies are cheerful,
Fairies are gold,
Fairies are secret,
Fairies are lovely.

Adele Mills (8)
Broadwater Down Primary School

BEING LEFT OUT

I hate school,
I feel like I'm all alone,
I'm always left in games
And never get spoken to.

I hate school,
All my friends don't like me as much,
When that girl came along,
I feel like I'm being let down.

I hate school,
I have no friends
And when I go home,
I can never forget my day at school.

Soumaya Selmi (10)
Broadwater Down Primary School

SPARKLE

Fireworks are dazzling,
Gold is nice,
Crystals are sparkly,
Silver can attract mice.

Stars are night,
Light is good,
Ice sparkles,
Diamonds are as strong as wood.

Fire is hot,
Lightning shakes you very much,
Rubies are fashion,
Sparklers hurt you with a touch.

Michael Gibbs (9)
Broadwater Down Primary School

SEASIDE

Look at my painting,
What do you see?
A person walking,
In the sea,
A long time ago.

Ladies sunbathing,
Men are waving,
People bathing,
Children waving.

Children sleeping,
Cats are eating,
People drinking,
Seagulls eating.

Sharna Smith (9)
Broadwater Down Primary School

OCEAN SAT UPON THE LAND

Ocean sat upon the land
Scaring all the people,
Reaching out his soggy hand.

The waves washed in near
With all the people's fear,
Then it flows back out again.

The surfers go out
And catch the waves
Then drift back in again.

Matthew Brooks (11)
Broadwater Down Primary School

RELATIVES

I have a strange aunty called Jean
She's quite tall and thin,
On bright sunny days,
She falls down the drain like a bean.

I have an uncle called Dean,
Who runs as fast as a stream,
On autumn days,
He runs as fast as a stream
My silly old uncle Dean.

I have a cousin called Kim,
Who turns as fast as the wind
On summer days,
She gets thinner and jumps
On two springs,
My silly old cousin Kim.

I have a brother called Jak,
He has a lot of plague,
On winter days
He flies to his friends,
My silly old brother Jak.

Michael Mills (10)
Broadwater Down Primary School

PLANTING AND DIGGING

Look in my painting,
People digging plants,
Out of the ground.

People galloping,
On their horses,
With jumble sale clothes.

Horses with hay,
On their backs,
People chasing sheep.

Into the field,
People with messy hands
And fingers.

Megan Stromeyer (9)
Broadwater Down Primary School

NONSENSE POEM

My dog is as fat as a rat,
My cat is lazy and sits on a mat,
My wizard is as daft as a monkey,
My family are chunky,
I know an alien 25 foot tall,
Who takes me to the mall,
If I know a seagull I would fly around
And I would sell a telephone for
One hundred pounds.

Katie Louise Gibbs (8)
Broadwater Down Primary School

POKÉMON

Pokémon is rough and tough,
On Pokémon Pikachu shot Bullbazor,
Kabatops sliced Onix the bonx.
Aerodactyl had a match without getting scratched,
Magmar burned Pikachu up,
Omastar got shell shocked by Pikachu,
Nidoking knocked out Nidoran.

Theo Chantler (7)
Broadwater Down Primary School

MY DOG

He is a big dog,
He likes to go for a jog,
He has sharp teeth,
He has teeth underneath,
His ears are straight like a gate,
He is black grey on his hairy legs.

Adam Selmi (8)
Broadwater Down Primary School

WHEN I GROW UP

When I grow up,
What shall I be?
Will I be different
Or still be me?

Sheree Ball (10)
Broadwater Down Primary School

TEACHER'S PET

I entered a competition,
To see if I could win,
I worked real hard to make things rhyme,
But could not think of a thing.

I took it into school next day
And put it in my tray,
The teacher had a read of it
And threw it all away.

I came home from school that day
Feeling quite upset,
I hope I win with this one,
As I am the teacher's pet.

Savannah Duffield (9)
Broadwater Down Primary School

MEMORIES OF HASTINGS

Seeing the seagulls, swooping and gliding,
Tasting the burger and chips in my mouth.

Smelling the fish and the salty sea water,
Feeling the old pebbles and broken crabs' legs.

Listening to waves rolling and crashing,
Listening to seagulls, screeching above.

Chloe Rusha (10)
Broadwater Down Primary School

BIRTHDAY

It was falling out of bed at the break of dawn.
It was challenging my brother to a pillow fight.
It was finding out my brother was too tired for words.
It was shaking my first birthday present.
It was saying, 'Yes!' To going to the Sea Life Centre in Hastings
                instead of going to the cinema and seeing Dinosaur.
It was going to Rusthall for Bonfire Night.
It was falling asleep in the back of the car on the way home.

Marie Gear (10)
Broadwater Down Primary School

I Wish

I wish I was a tree
So I would be climbed.
I wish I was a dog
So I would get stroked.
I wish I was a fence
So I could wobble.
I wish I was a mayor
So I could boss people about.

Tim Gear (8)
Broadwater Down Primary School

River

The river is calm
And ever so cold,
It's seen many things
Because it's very old.
It's seen thunder and lightning,
Storms and rain,
Over and over and over again.
I'm in my boat
And as we float,
I hear birds singing
And church bells ringing,
And children playing on the banks,
Laughing and jumping, pulling pranks,
I hear a horn blow,
It's time to go,
Goodbye to all.

Lace Murphy (9)
Colyers Primary School

WHY CAN'T THEY BE FREE

Why can't they be free?
Like the birds in the tree.
Why can't they be free?
Like the fish in the sea.
Why can't they be free?
Like the honey-making bee.
Why can't they be free?
Like the dolphin with such glee.
Why can't they be free?
Like the dog-loving flea.
Why can't they be free?
Like you and me.

Please let them be free.

Imogen Ross (9)
Colyers Primary School

HAMSTERS

Running and running on their wheel,
Travelling nowhere fast,
The only time it seems to stop,
Is for a gulp or bite to eat,
Their smooth, shiny coat,
So ginger and white,
They keep you amused for weeks.

Joe Shaw (10)
Colyers Primary School

A JOURNEY THROUGH LIFE

A homeless old man,
So weary and cold,
Begging for money,
As he grows old.

A homeless old man,
Roaming the street,
A melancholy face,
With little to eat.

Thinking back through his life,
As a child, as a boy,
Spending time with his parents
And playing with toys.

And back to his wedding day
Holding his bride
And the birth of his first born,
His face full of pride.

His son starts work,
When his work now must end,
He looses his wife
And many of his friends.

A homeless old man,
With his arms open wide,
Takes his journey to Heaven
With his wife by his side.

Jasmine O'Neill (10)
Downe Primary School

FOOTBALL FEVER

I love going to footy games with my dad,
Standing in the terraces I feel so glad,
Waiting with anticipation for my team to score,
Singing all the football songs, listening for the roar.

'One-nil Millwall.'

All I see is their keeper lying on the floor,
The Millwall fans are filled with awe,
The ball is on the centre spot,
Have the opposition read the plot?

All you hear, around the ground, are the cheers,
'Bring it on we have no fears'
Now the ref blows, to signal the end
And I can't wait to come again.

My team has won.

Max Saville (11)
Downe Primary School

OLIVER

My cat Oliver is a tabby,
He is very old and very scraggy,
He sleeps on my bed every night,
His left ear is torn from a recent fight.
Since he was little, he has no tail,
But when catching mice, he never fails
And when each day comes to an end
I know that Oliver is my best friend.

Abigail Phillips (10)
Downe Primary School

NO ONE MAN

There he stands,
Alone and untouched,
Loneliness becomes of him,
Thy power cannot hurt him,
Thy words cannot harm,
Thy promises and hopes cannot heal him.

There he stands,
Scared of what might happen,
He writes letters to nobody,
He asks questions at no one,
The world is nothing to him,
Thy sayings and phrases cannot help.

There he stands,
He does not mourn with despair,
He does not excel with joy,
He does not sense that he has no life to live,
His body is just an empty space.

He is just a no one man.

Michael Lever (9)
Downe Primary School

THE SOLAR SYSTEM

Mercury is hot,
Pluto is cold,
Earth has life,
So we are told.

The sun is the centre,
Giving energy and light,
Saturn and Venus shimmer,
Beautiful and bright.

Mars the red planet,
With deserts and mountains,
Uranus and Neptune gases twirling and
Bouncing.

Jupiter the biggest, it says in my book,
But the moon is my favourite,
Each night in my telescope I look!

Aaron Farron (11)
Downe Primary School

DO THEY REALLY CARE?

Litter, litter everywhere,
Do these people really care,
About our damaged world?

Pollution, factories everywhere,
Do these people really care,
About the life of this world?

Hunting, farming everywhere,
Do these people really care,
About the wildlife of this world?

Famine, war everywhere,
Do these people really care,
About the children of this world?

Murder, crime everywhere,
Do these people really care,
About each other?

Emma Grant (10)
Downe Primary School

My Dumb Dog

Sitting there shaking and quivering you'd think he's terrified,
As a squirrel scurries past on the fence post right outside.

Lying there, legs outstretched, looking like a king,
One minute so regal, until he hears the doorbell ring.

Saturday morning and I think 'Great a chance to lie in bed,'
Then before I know it, there's a heavy lump upon my leg.

Taking the dog for a walk isn't always fun,
We can't let him off the lead because we know he'll never come.

He's a very greedy dog, he'll eat anything in sight,
Once he licked a plate of vindaloo which gave him quite a fright.

Of all the things he does and the things that drive me mad,
I know to have a dog like Bertie is the best thing I've ever had.

Grace Perry (10)
Downe Primary School

The Titanic

T he Titanic sets sail on the ocean blue,
H ooray chants the crowd, wish we were with you.
E veryone watches the liner fade away.

T he time is late, the ship gently sways,
I ceberg, iceberg the lookout screams,
T he captain feels his ship comes apart at the seams
A nd then comes the panic,
N o one knows what to think,
I s this the impossible?
C ould we possibly sink?

Ryan Sadler (9)
Downe Primary School

FLYING

As I travelled through the air,
The chilling breeze went through my hair,
Twisting, turning until I fall,
I hope I won't descend at all,
Trees and plants rocking to and fro,
Watching them swing and watching them grow,
The clouds were all that were in sight,
A sudden gust gave me a fright,
Suddenly I began to fall,
I wondered if this was real at all,
The clouds got wet, cold and grey,
I suppose I will have to wait for another day,
I wish I could just fly away.

Adam Young (9)
Downe Primary School

WINTER

W e are cold on winter days,
    But we like to laugh and play.
I n the snow we skate and ski
    Children run wild and free
N ice and warm by the fireside,
    All the creatures always hide.
T he fish swim in the frozen pond,
    The robin still sings its happy song.
E ating lots on Christmas Day,
    We have visitors come and stay.
R udolph reindeer led the way,
    Pulling Santa's pretty sleigh.

Erin Gilbrook (9)
Downe Primary School

Do You Roast?

We crossed the Atlantic on Thursday,
Our jumbo was big and red,
It is such a long way,
I wish I'd stayed in bed.

When we got there, it was sunny
And the sea was warm as toast,
I know you will think this is funny,
But I felt like a Sunday roast.

In Disney we went to stay,
It was really great,
We stayed for two weeks and a day
And there we met a new mate.

His name was Micky Mouse
And we had our picture taken,
We visited him in his house,
He gave us eggs and bacon.

I would have really preferred a roast,
But Minnie did not know what to do,
Now, I am not one to boast,
But I know how to, do you?

Natasha Sikora (11)
Downe Primary School

MOON OR MARS?

We went on a school trip up to Mars,
We brought lots of drink
And plenty of bars.

Twix, Bounty and Maltesers too,
My friend couldn't come,
She had the flu.

I brought some clothes and loads of cash,
I admired our rocket,
It was rather flash!

We stopped at the moon for a Coke and the loo,
But unfortunately for me,
I got stuck in the queue.

But while I was waiting unbeknown,
They had jumped in the rocket
And off they had flown.

I wish I wasn't the only one,
Waiting and waiting,
For the next school trip to come.

I'm not afraid, I have no fear,
I just hope,
I get home some time this year!

Katie Beard (11)
Downe Primary School

THE JOURNEY

I'm going to a planet far away,
The Earth I'm leaving behind,
Launch date is one day away,
The rest of my time is blind.

The ship is set on course for Mars,
I'm on automatic pilot,
I'm cruising through the stars,
I'm going crazy but I don't mind it.

Everything in space is still and in it I float,
I'm weightless within an invisible boat,
My destiny is in the stars,
My life begins when I dock on Mars.

Freddie Chandler Darlison (11)
Downe Primary School

LIFE

Life can be happy, life can be sad,
Life can be fun, life can be bad,
Life can be short, life can be long,
Life can be sweet, like a bird's song.

Some eyes are blue, some eyes are brown,
Everybody can cry or frown,
It doesn't matter what you do or wear,
Even if people stop and stare.

It doesn't matter if you are dumb or smart,
What matters is what's in the heart!

Amy Schofield (10)
Downe Primary School

A DAY AT THE BEACH

Look at the gleaming, golden sand,
It makes you touch it with your hand,
Building castles, throughout the day,
Watch the people run and play.

The deep blue sea appears like crystal,
What could possibly make you miserable?
Jolly families rowing their boats,
Leaving foamy ripples as they float.

A traditional lunch of fish and chips,
For others, it's tortillas and dips,
Don't forget the ice cream sundae
And finish off with a can of 'fizzy' eh?

Then for the parents, a nap in the sun,
Whilst the kids just have some fun,
Night is descending, watch them retreat,
Back to their homes and a good night's sleep!

Rachel Munn (11)
Fordcombe CE Primary School

MY CAT

I love my cat,
His name is Matt,
He is orange and white
And miaows at night
But I still love my cat.

Jonathan Passmore (9)
Fordcombe CE Primary School

POP

Pop bands from A to Z,
A1, Steps and all the rest,
Number ones around the world,
Loads of singles and albums sold,
Boy bands, girl bands, some are mixed,
Some dance slow and some dance quick,
Some bands really try their best,
Their fans really put them to the test,
So who do you think is the best,
Westlife, Spice Girls or maybe, Steps,
Earning lots of money, doing very well,
Depending of course on how much music they sell,
As concerts finish and CDs end,
Off go the fans with broken hearts to mend.

Lindsay Smith (11)
Fordcombe CE Primary School

BONFIRE NIGHT

Bang! Bang!

Rockets in the air,
Leaving behind a big bright flare.

Whizz! Whizz!

All the children squeal
As they saw the light of the Catherine wheel.

Pop! Pop!

The crowd went mad,
The fire went out, so they were sad.

Alex Williams (10)
Fordcombe CE Primary School

YIPPEE SCHOOL'S OUT

The school bells ring, ring, ring,
To all the children it will bring, bring, bring,
Register time, children bustle,
While you hear the bags rustle,
Literacy lesson goes quite well,
Till they hear the break time bell,
Art comes after break,
A boat is what the children make,
When the lunchtime arrives,
It brings lots of sighs,
Stomachs are full,
Now it's time to play ball,
Time flies by,
While they learn about the sky,
The end of the day,
We stop quickly to pray.
Yippee school's out!

Patrick Peel-Barnard (8)
Fordcombe CE Primary School

THE OLYMPICS

I love the Olympics,
They come every four years,
Rowing, boxing, track and field altogether,
Are so great,
They may be fun for us to watch,
The athletes must try so hard,
After all their only aim is to go for gold,

All in all I think that the Olympics are the best thing yet.

Jack Hill (10)
Fordcombe CE Primary School

WAR

Bombs big,
Bombs small.

Grenades are handled,
Call them all.

The army injured,
The army strong.

Ethiopia against
Hong Kong.

Who will win,
We don't know.

Let's go, go, go!

Rilly Stookes (8)
Fordcombe CE Primary School

THE PARK

Leaves rustle,
People bustle.

Twigs snap,
Coats flap.

Swings ping,
Birds sing.

Kites fly,
Babies cry.

Children gaze,
Happy days.

Jack Stookes (10)
Fordcombe CE Primary School

THE BATTLE OF HASTINGS

The Papal banner flapped in the air,
As William of Normandy's archers advanced,
Firing volleys of arrows as they went.

Then came the charge of the knight,
Up Senalac Hill, towards King Harold's Saxons
But the English soldiers held firm.

The Housecarls swung their axes,
Dehorsing many a Norman knight,
The Duke's men turned and retreated,
When they saw their Lord had fallen.

But Duke William climbed back into his saddle,
Raised his helmet and
Rallied his troops.

The Saxons had chased their retreating foes,
Shouting terrible war cries,
They just couldn't be stopped.

By the time William's army had regrouped,
The Saxons were at the bottom of the hill
And pushing forwards.

The Saxon's king, Harold, was killed,
He was hit in the eye with an arrow
And stabbed in the chest with a sword.

Douglas Johnson (10)
Harenc School

THE ALPHABET WAR

A is for air rifle firing at the soldiers,
B is for bombs being dropped from the sky,
C is for commandos creeping silently along the ground,
D is for democratic plans to kill the enemy,
E is for entering the foe's base, waiting to strike,
F is for fast action to be taken,
G is for guns being shot, not knowing if you have hit,
H is for harpoons being blown,
I is for inflicting damage to their buildings,
J is for jagged knives with sharp points,
K is for knowing where to hide and what to do,
L is for land mines being planted in the ground,
M is for masters fighting with their bare hands,
N is for the night, the soldier carries on,
O is for old people fearing the war,
P is for parachuters jumping from planes,
Q is for questions being asked to the hostages,
R is for riots started by religion and whose land it is,
S is for the sound of the trigger being pulled,
T is for tampering with the bombs,
U is for underground battles happening at the time,
V is for velocity of the bombs being dropped,
W is for walls being blown to the ground,
X is for Xmas when the warriors come home,
Y is for year book, telling everyone about their war,
Z is for zany people on the enemies' side.

George Sullivan (10)
Harenc School

OTT

My name is Large and I come from planet Mars,
I used to live in the dump but it awfully
Stunk so I moved to Harenc School.

When I arrived at the school, the children thought
I was a fool, so I decided to hide in the sink.

I am three foot four so I am quite close to
The floor and my favourite colour is pink.

I have three blood-shot eyes
Which are not very nice to look at in the night.
They drip with blood but often flood,
So I know and then have to fill them with mud.

School dinners are sick but not according to Nick,
He scrapes the plates clean giving them a sparkling sheen.

I am totally rubbish at sums but I don't mind
Playing with toy guns,
English is a blast but Miss says I read too fast.

I had two tentacles near my waist but the
Children thought they were fake,
So they pulled them off and I died and
Went to planet Moff.

Christopher Nelson (10)
Harenc School

HAUNTED HOUSE

I stepped in the house
With a frightened look,
I'm screaming inside my body
And I can feel fear.
I had a peep round a door
And saw a funny looking chair
And a strange chandelier shaking.

I crept out of the room and
Looked around and saw a flicker
Of a weird looking light.
There was a shiver going down my spine.
This meant I was really frightened and
Not knowing what to do next.
I thought it would be better to check it out,
Now I thought this is getting very creepy.

I crept in the room and saw a green slimy monster
Which had red bulging eyes.
The revolting monster saw me,
I thought I was going to faint any second,
The monster was about to grab me,
But then I woke up,
All sweaty and breathless.

Rishi Chopra (9)
Harenc School

PENCIL CASE

Pencil case, stencil race, pencil fight, sharpener's bite,
Sharpener's waste, rubber's paste, Tippex leaves without a trace.

Colouring pencils, essential stencils, water-based pen,
The newest trend, pencil sharpenings, still heightening.

Ruler, protractor, calculator, they're all maths
Fact finders, put in a ring binder.

Fountain pen, biro's friend, fountain pen,
Eraser makes the paper smell sickening on end.

Lessons at the end, oh look there's my pen.

Siulun Ko (10)
Harenc School

THE WEATHER IS NEVER THE SAME

Sixty million years back in the past,
Dinosaurs were predicting the weather forecast,
Texas was hit by a comet,
Which made all the dinosaurs vomit.

Early man thought there would be sun,
Which they thought was real fun,
Next day there was torrential rain,
That turned out to be a real pain.

The Arctic was bitterly chilly,
Which drove all the penguins silly,
Most were eaten by a polar bear,
Who had to catch them with great care.

In the US they were hit by a tornado,
Which made a house look like play dough,
It caught a bus, car and lorry,
A basket, roof and shopping trolley.

The UK were experiencing a storm,
Which electrocuted barley and shredded corn,
Farmer's mad, their field's not the same,
The weather is a real pain.

Alexander Whitehead (11)
Harenc School

WHEN WE'RE AT THE SHOPPING MALL

When we're at the shopping mall, there always is disaster,
My brother, at messing, is definitely the master,
First we hit the sports shop,
My brother's favourite,
He messes around with the football tops thinking he's a pro.

Secondly the book shop, oh no more disaster,
As I said, at messing up, my brother's easily the best,
First all the pages go rip,
Then the pens and pencils go crack
And finally the manager goes chatting with our mum, blab, blab, blab,
Naughty, naughty, naughty.

Lastly the food,
Oh dear the worst place to be when my brother's around,
I'll have to add more lines to the poem,
When we open the door there's always a scream of joy,
He's not happy for receiving a free toy,
It's a big food fight he can't wait for,
There's the chips which soar through the sky like missiles,
Burgers flying like spaceships
And Coke spitting and spilling like poison acid, a mad fight,
But after all it's us who got into major trouble - doh!

Vincent Law (10)
Harenc School

COMPUTERS

Computers are brain boxes,
They hold statements and documents,
All the numbers and money
That people have saved.

Computer games played
By children, get lots of
Fun out of them.

Writing stories on the keyboard,
Takes a long time to write
Because I take a long time.

So that is what a computer does,
Computers are magnificent things.

Matthew Ody (10)
Harenc School

IN THE LOFT

Up there in the loft,
   I'm sure that there
Up in the loft,
   Is a huge monster!

The monster is orange,
   With bulging cheeks,
Each side of his large head,
   He smells like dead meat.

He is as big as four houses,
   It has four eyes, mouths, noses
And even strips of hair!
   It's name is Fourn.

When everyone has gone to sleep,
   He blows his collected nightmares,
Into your head!
   This is where nightmares come from.

My mum says that this isn't true,
It is
I tell her,
It is as true as it gets.

Jeremy Dodd (10)
Harenc School

SCHOOL DINNERS

As you walk to the diner,
You can smell all those yucky smells,
The lumpy custard,
The lovely mustard.

The sausages are horrible,
The gravy's adorable.
In the queue,
You can see the green goo
Of the smelly jelly.

After we've had our food,
We come to the pud,
Lumpy custard is not good,
The lovely sponge cake,
But I think it's fake.

It's time to line up,
I've got to go to class.

It's the end of lunch!

Joseph Kington (10)
Harenc School

TOGIMAHIGE

Beware of the Togimahige
Its teeth are as sharp as razor blades,
Its nails cut like a butcher's knife,
His eyes are as bulged as huge balloons,
His tail is a twisted helter skelter,
His tongue is as sticky as superglue,
He mumbles to himself, 'Soon I'm going to eat you.'

His favourite food is the Slaki bird,
He finds it high in the tree,
He takes it back to his den
And eats it very fast indeed.

If this is just my imagination,
I wonder what a dream world would be like?

Daniel Timcke (9)
Harenc School

WHEN I AM DREAMING

When I am dreaming I can roam free in any place in the world,
When I can lay down and look at the clouds,
Forming different shapes and sizes,
When I can play football, rugby, tennis or any
Particular sport I want.

When I am dreaming, I can get an autograph
From anybody in the world,
I can see any play or video,
When I am dreaming, I can watch Friends,
My favourite TV show, all day.

When I am dreaming, I can go to sleep and
Get up in a year or two,
When I can get a good education without
Learning about anything.

When I can have a feast every day of the week.

When I am dreaming, I can do anything,
When I am dreaming, everything is my delusion.

Joshua Ott (9)
Harenc School

THE KNIGHT

Galloping through the autumn breeze,
Comes a knight,
A knight clad in shining armour,
With a sword by his side,
He has been sent by God to bring peace to the world.

Riding across the land he comes,
Ridding the land of greedy ogres and deadly dragons,
People cheer him as he canters through the towns,
'Long live the knight,' they would cry.

Onto the crusades he went,
Bringing many victories,
Against the Saracen armies
As he did his duty for God.

Galloping towards the horizon,
Goes the knight,
On his way to bring peace,
To a world ruled by greed and hate.

Julian Dix (10)
Harenc School

THE LIGHTNING BOLT

The lightning bolt strikes the house,
Breaks the tiles and scares the mouse.

The lightning bolts strikes the tree,
Burning it down as small as a flea.

The lightning bolt strikes the train,
Makes it crash and causes great pain.

The lightning bolt strikes the farm,
Bringing sadness and great harm.

The lightning bolt strikes the church,
Which killed the bird that fell off its perch.

The lightning bolt strikes the school,
Bringing joy to all the pupils,
Hooray.

Gino Ferrara (9)
Harenc School

THE CLEANER

I'm two foot four, I'm close to the floor,
That's why I clean to make it gleam,
Once I had a job to clean a boat's deck,
But a person threw a pea which knocked me into the sea.

Then I was a cook but I was no good at that,
So now I write books,
My brother is a crook,
I'm not very proud of him
But I like my other brother Tim,
Even though he is dim.

My mum is called Karen,
She works at a tavern,
My dad is called Paul,
He makes stools,
He is very cool.

Luke Powis (10)
Harenc School

A CHRISTMAS POEM

C hristmas is the happy time of year, everyone is dancing
   and praising Lord Jesus' birthday.
H appy children and parents are opening their
   presents before Christmas dinner.
R ich Christmas cakes are being eaten before
   everyone waits till midnight.
I cy cold snowmen are built in back gardens,
   smiling through the windows at all the people inside.
S hiny faces as boys and girls wake up to their full stockings,
T urkey all golden brown and delicious, is laid on
   the table soon to be eaten.
M ummies and daddies fall asleep in front of the TV,
   late at night, thinking it's not Christmas for another year.
A unties and uncles come to visit at Christmas
   and if they don't, the thought is there.
S pring is near and new babies of all animals are on their way.

Thomas McNally (10)
Harenc School

MY HOBBIES

My favourite sport is cricket,
Although football is pretty good,
I'd rather hit the middle wicket,
Than do my homework which I should.

Cycling is a hobby of mine,
I like the breeze through my hair,
I can barely go in a straight line,
But do I really care?

I go to scouts which is great fun,
We play 'Man Hunt' in the trees,
I can never catch anyone,
Maybe next time God please.

It's time to finish up this rhyme,
I know it wasn't the best,
Maybe it'll be better next time,
So now I'd better get dressed.

Charlie Bown (11)
Harenc School

I DON'T WANT TO GO TO SCHOOL

I don't want to go to school,
I want to play football all day long
And watch TV at home.

I don't want to go to school,
I don't want to do homework all night,
I want to play computer games.

I don't want to go to school,
I know more than the teacher's know,
So I don't have to do work.

I don't want to go to school,
I don't have to do all these tests because I'm clever,
I don't need books to learn from,
I can work them out in seconds.

Only joking - not!

Alain Wilkinson (9)
Harenc School

LUNCHTIME QUEUE

Down in my tummy, I'm feeling so hungry,
My mind is on nothing but lovely food.

What's on the menu today,
Let me imagine what it might say.

There's tagliatelli with cheese which is smelly,
To fill up my belly when I'm in the mood.

There's strawberry fruit cakes with cream like my mum makes,
You don't know what it takes all afternoon.

I'll tell you what's on the menu,
It's cottage pie or stew,
Cook has been busy all morning,
She's cooked some lovely food.

Lewis Harjani (10)
Harenc School

IF THERE WAS NO SCHOOL TODAY

If there was no school today,
I'd scream and shout and play all day.

I'd stay at home and mess with clay.

I'd phone my friend and talk all day
About my teacher, Miss May.

I'd drink lots of Fanta,
Go and meet Santa.

I'd eat lots of sweets, go on treats.
I'd stay in my warm bed all day
But that's a shame I'm going to school today.

Kit Bradshaw (10)
Harenc School

WHAT I FIND IN THE PARK!

A soggy box,
A cunning fox,
A bully larking,
A doggy barking,
Footballs darting,
My uncle Martin,
People running far,
A smashed jam jar,
People having fun,
Joggers on the run,
A smelly bin,
Banana skin,
This is what I find in the park,
But not when it's dark.

Charles Sunley (9)
Harenc School

LAMBEATER 2: JUDGEMENT DAY

Oh no!
The scientists have made a genetically modified
Lambeater!
Is he coming this way
Or are people in the North Atlantic asking him to stay?
Is he very powerful
Or is he like a piece of wood?
Does he have three eyes?
Does he tell lies?
Does he have five fingers?
Or does he have smelly toes that linger?
I don't know who he is
And I hope he does not come this way.

Gopun Jani (9)
Harenc School

THE PILOT BUG

The Pilot Bug was brave and calm,
When swooping through the air,
But, when he was upon the ground
There was a hassle everywhere,
What was that funny sound he thought?
While climbing from his plane
A crash and bang of feet and hands
And people squealing out his name
'He's here, he's here' the people cried
For they had thought their Pilot Bug had died,
'What is the time?' the bug enquired.
'Oh yes, it's half past nine'
He got into a blue cocoon and slept a little while,
When he awoke with purple wings,
He threw away his plane
And so it is till this very day, a butterfly he became.

Maddie Spence (8)
Lady Boswell's CE Primary School

THE SUN

The sun,
The sun,
It's like a big fat bun,
Although it can run,
It's still the sun,
It's glowing light, illuminates the sky,
But when it gets late, it says goodbye,
That is how we get our nights,
The sun,
The sun,
Has great delights.

Tamsira Nwitua (10)
Parkway Primary School

THE SUN

Gradually the sun rises from its bed,
Passing the dark gloomy old houses,
Waking everyone from their beds,
Arms wide with a dark yellow, fat face,
Yellow fingers touching the old houses,
It passes the gardens and it makes all the flowers stand up,
Out from the alleyway to the nice green fields,
It touches the grass and makes it all start talking,
When it's hot, it starts getting angry,
Shouting, shouting,
Getting very annoyed with other people,
Screaming, screaming,
It makes all the little ones cry,
It went to sleep and woke up the next morning,
Happy and cheerful,
It goes to the beach,
Makes everyone hot and thirsty,
He goes home to his family.

Charlotte Barnard (11)
Parkway Primary School

THE SUN

The sun appears in the morning like a fireball in the sky,
Like a happy child,
That goes to sleep during the night,
His blazing face giving the Earth light,
Its blinding light touching the equator,
Shining through the windows from the crack of dawn,
Flickering and glimmering from,
Shining and sparkling,
Like a man hunting all the darkness.

Charlie Curtis (10)
Parkway Primary School

THE RAIN

Heavily it rains,
Mean faces in the droplets,
Splashing all over the path,
The faces looking for someone to hit,
Past the wet gardens
And when it reaches the ground,
You can hear a little scream,
Down from the sky at 1000 mph,
Heavily it rains,
Splashing and showering,
The mean faces are getting worse,
Spraying, plunging,
On the windows of the houses,
Heavily, it rains,
Will this horror ever stop?

Luke Ballard (11)
Parkway Primary School

THE THING

It might be red,
It might be blue,
It could be anything
Even you.

It was in the school,
But not in the hall,
It was really smelly,
But not made of jelly.

Oh what a terrible thing.

Leela Homewood (9)
Parkway Primary School

THE STORM

It's a peaceful and quiet day,
The sun's shining in the bay,
People making sandcastles
And the sun just hustles and bustles.

When the sun goes down and the sky is black,
Everyone runs with sacks on their backs,
The heavy rain starts pouring down
And soon the long storm comes to town.

The storm soon spreads and howls like a wolf,
It moves around hunting for food,
The big, fat storm gets bigger and bigger
And soon the big storm comes to town.

The storm finds out there is no food,
Killing the town would bring him no good,
It travels somewhere very quickly
And gets out of town very angrily.

The storm gets out of town.

Kukua Asihene (10)
Parkway Primary School

THE RAIN

Slowly the rain starts to spit,
Then cries and stops getting angry and strikes,
Slowly but surely it floods streets,
Surrounded by water,
Then slowly, slowly stops.

Dean Day (10)
Parkway Primary School

FALLING ASLEEP!

In the dark, cold bedroom, I'm lying in my bed,
The events of the day all twirling round in my brainy head,
It is a school day tomorrow and at seven o'clock
It will be time to get up,
Downstairs the smell of bacon and eggs
Cooking on the stove.
I'm looking forward to nice, hot chocolate
In my special dog cup,
The fresh summer smell, the lavender
Opening up, all pretty and all mauve.
Now the day is over,
The spotted cows all eating spread out clover,
Back to bed I go,
In the kitchen my mum making lovely dough,
Quietly one rustle of a quilt
I fall fast asleep once again today,
Tomorrow will be the first of May.

Katie Frost (9)
Perry Hall Primary School

THE TEDDY BEAR

I was walking through the park one night
And saw a teddy bear,
I said 'Hello there, young chap, why are you sitting there?'
And he replied, 'I'm cold and I think I've broken my leg,
So can you take me home tonight and put me in your bed?
My favourite food is scrambled egg and my best friend was
Betty Peg, but now you've found me sitting here, you
Are my best friend instead.'

Amie Arthrell (12) & Hope Watson (11)
Perry Hall Primary School

FALLING ASLEEP

In the night, warm and snuggled in my bed,
I hear the rowdy guys come,
The drunk, angry fist into someone else's face.
When it happens, the selfish, inconsiderate laugh of the crowd,
One thing I think whenever I hear this, I wonder why they have it.
The alcohol and the non-stop rattling of glass bottles,
Then constantly throwing them at vehicles,
Screeching when it breaks.
The house next door, the builders love snoring,
I think it is their favourite habit,
As the evening turns to night, the television goes off
And the lights go out, the whole house finally sleeps,
I drop off into a deep sleep, wondering what the next day will bring.

Matthew Roche (10)
Perry Hall Primary School

FALLING ASLEEP

I'm falling, softly down and down,
Hearing voices moving from room to room,
The doors squeaking while opening,
Slam when they close,
The radiator rumbling and gurgling,
Outside the distant sound of people shouting, drunk,
The wind whistling, the rain pounding, the window
Wanting to come in,
The broken street lamp flickering on and off,
Buzzing a bit like a bee,
The moon shines like a firefly in a big long jar,
Everything clears and goes,
I'm falling, falling asleep.

Victoria Purcell (10)
Perry Hall Primary School

SHORT DAYS AND LONG NIGHTS!

Sleep, sleep,
I do not like
I wish I could stay up all night,
I don't want to snuggle up so tight,
I go to the furthest level in my game,
Goodnight I hear in dear vain.

Sleep, sleep,
I do not like it
When I am in my bed,
I hate being bothered in my head,
All the noises keep me awake,
Especially my hamster on its whirly plate.

Sleep, sleep,
I do not like
Fading in the cold dark night,
Please do leave me alone,
I'm drifting . . .

Jurrell Bromfield (9)
Perry Hall Primary School

A TROPICAL ISLAND . . . I WISH!

I wish a tropical island was mine,
I'd have a bar, serving cocktails and wine,
I'd lay on the beach and soak up the sun,
Then I'd splash in the sea and have some fun,
The crabs would come to play with me
And dolphins would invite me around to tea,
A bit unreal, this may seem
But everyone's got to have a dream . . .

Emma Shiel (11)
Perry Hall Primary School

DAYDREAM

I daydream, I daydream,
Should I be in class?
I don't know but I do know,
That class is boring,
All we do is English, Maths
And science,
It's all boring to me.

Do you like class, I don't!

I daydream, I daydream,
I daydream about different lands,
I daydream about my favourite animals
And I still daydream in class!

Do you daydream in class?
I do!

Helena Brett (9)
Perry Hall Primary School

SEEING THE LIGHT

I was out in the cold
I was hungry and thirsty,
I wanted to see you in the distance
The mist was thick and white like snow.
I see a glistening light
From a far house
I saw the warmth coming
Out of the window
Coming to greet me in my bed.

Rebekah Day (9)
Perry Hall Primary School

IN THE DARKNESS I LAY

In the darkness I lay,
I can't sleep,
The day running through my head,
Moments at a time.

In the darkness I lay,
Noises all around me,
Creeping closer.

In the darkness I lay,
My eyes are getting heavy,
As I come towards the next day
Drifting,
Drifting
Away.

Sadie Whitlock (10)
Perry Hall Primary School

FALLING ASLEEP

The distant sound of rustling trees;
The pigeons soaring to find shelter for the long, bitter night;
The stars glistening like diamonds on a sheet of black velvet;
The evening star hanging above the horizon;
The harsh hail whipping the ground;
And the fire still burning, blending with
December air;
This Christmas Eve, I'm listening for the faint jingle
of sleighbells in cool air.
The world fading into peace.

David Poulter (10)
Perry Hall Primary School

FALLING ASLEEP

The screams of the foxes
Drip, drip of the tap next door,
Creaking of floorboards.
The glimmering moon outside,
The TV blaring out downstairs.
Twinkling silver stars around the pale moon.
Small thuds of people around me,
The chit chat of parents discussing
The day's events.
A ginger cat miaowing in the distance
The aggressive dog, barking ferociously.
A lost rabbit looking for food,
The yells from the next-door neighbours.
I'm slowly falling asleep.

Emily Perry (9)
Perry Hall Primary School

FALLING ASLEEP

The tap is dripping softly in the quiet house
It is cold whilst I am under the warmest covers ever.
A police car's siren wailing in the distance
Clattering noises of dustbin lids falling off in the darkness
The creaking of doors when the wind pushes it.
Cars zooming by, further and further into the distance.
My swing is rocking when a gust of wind touches it
The television is on, chatting away to itself.
A sudden light hits me smack in the face.
It is warm whilst I fall asleep.
Goodnight.

Daniel Moriarty (9)
Perry Hall Primary School

FALLING ASLEEP

Voices in a silent night,
The television showing films,
Making a chatting sound,
The dog tapping up the stairs,
Talking, all from downstairs,
I can't go to sleep.
I dare say I wish these noises would go away.
Next-door shouting all night,
The foxes are looking for their food,
People shouting along the street,
Going out for trick or treat.
The trees are whispering,
In the black night,
Now it is midnight,
Everything has gone dead now,
I can have peace and dreams.

Spencer Beale (10)
Perry Hall Primary School

PICTURES IN THE FIRE

In the fire I see pictures of things,
They dance about us as the fire glows,
It draws me far, far away,
I wonder if I will ever see the light of day.

It takes me to distant lands,
Magical things to see
But it's all in my head
And I wish I could dream it in bed,
I wish you could see what I could see.

Rachel Lewis (10)
Perry Hall Primary School

SOFT AND SQUIDGY

I'm as white as a sheep,
Far up there,
White and fluffy,
In the air.

I'm as soft as a tissue,
As well as white,
I'm only seen in the light.

I come in all different shapes,
As well as sizes,
I am proud
Because I'm a cloud.

Kristi Cormack & Chanel Olivia Brown (9)
Perry Hall Primary School

I'M WAKING UP

I'm waking up from my
siesta on a cold autumn month.
The leaves on the oak tree
the crisp winter morning
wrinkled leaves falling off
their wooden finger.
The slippery leaves in the
wood and a path that takes
me into the unknown.
Then I rise from my dream
in a place that I know.

I'm waking up.

Sam Newstead (9)
Perry Hall Primary School

TRYING TO GET TO SLEEP

I woke up in my soft cold bed,
staring at the walls.
I had such a bad dream last night,
I didn't get a wink of sleep.
as I heard the dog next door
It made me wonder if I would ever drift off again.
As I tried to doze off, all I could do was stay awake.
I was so cold so I went to the window
hoping the radiator would come on.
I looked out of the window and guess what I saw
The bright shining lamp from the house next door.
As I stared at the flickering light in the darkness,
I could feel the warmth coming to me.
From the distance, I could see the slow, red, rising sun.
So I went back to bed, and suddenly fell asleep.

Tanya Sanderson (9)
Perry Hall Primary School

I AM SITTING IN MY TABBY OLD CHAIR

I am sitting in my tabby old chair, sleeping, dreaming,
My whole body in a deep, deep slumber,
Of silence,
My brain is the seven seas of dreams,
Where my soul is I don't have a clue,
But where I am, is sitting in my tabby old
Chair sleeping, dreaming
And when I wake I would have sailed
All the seven seas of dreams.

Kate Mills (10)
Perry Hall Primary School

THE DRAGON HEADMASTER

I think the head teacher is nice.
He has long green feet
But that doesn't bother me.
With a big spooky tail
That trails the ground
I don't know how he gets
The scratch marks on the wall.
It is very hot inside it
Can sometimes cloud the windows.
But I can't see his face
Because I am just a mouse
Who is only four inches tall
And I wonder why children
Are so afraid of him.

Samantha Hare (8)
Perry Hall Primary School

MY DREAM

I am walking up a hill
I am tired
I am rolling down the hill
I am stuck on the edge
I am crying for help
I can hear my heart thumping loudly
Suddenly
I am sitting up in bed
With my mum and dad beside me.

Bethany Hedges (9)
Perry Hall Primary School

THE MOON

I want to fly to the moon,
In a great big balloon,
I want to jump through
The stars and land,
Stop on Mars
To invite a Martian
Home to tea.
What a great
Idea that would be
And when it was time to go
We would fly past Jupiter
And Pluto,
Waving at Venus
And Mercury too,
That is the adventure,
That I would like to do.

Janine James (7)
Perry Hall Primary School

FALLING ASLEEP

The rustling of trees outside in the freezing cold
The repeating drip of the bathroom tap.
A creak of a floorboard outside the door.
What on earth was that?
Foxes screaming
A wolf's whine.
The rain thudding on my window
A wild black cat in the distance
The scuffle of a rat.
Can I ever properly fall asleep?

Sophie Brett (9)
Perry Hall Primary School

A BIT LONGER

I'm in bed watching TV
I can hear the sizzling of the cooker
And the thump of my heart
When an exciting part comes up
'Turn the TV off!'
'A bit longer,' I say.
The creaking of the floorboards
Makes a cold icy shiver up my back.
'Turn the TV off!'
'Okay,' I reply to my mum.
The boiler hums, I freeze
and I'm gone.

Harry Johnson (10)
Perry Hall Primary School

FALLING ASLEEP

Angry foxes scream
Aggressive dogs barking.
The soft drip of a tap
The creaking floorboards of the stairs.
The flashing headlights of passing
cars through the curtains.
The humungus crash of the
television on below
The crash of the dustbins by the
strong gales outside.
The massive roar of an aeroplane's engine.

Andrew Millis (9)
Perry Hall Primary School

FALLING ASLEEP

My puppy whining all night long, on and on
However can I get to *sleep?*

How about counting sheep?
One sheep, two sheep, three sheep
That won't help me get to sleep!
My mind is going in a whizz!
How about reading The Fizz?

I think about getting a drink
I can, Dad's watching The Weakest Link.
I can't get to sleep I've tried counting sheep!
Owls hooting and lurking in the tree
I don't know how, but they can *see me!*

I think of a ballerina on the stage
I'll bet she gets lots of wages
Mum, I'm in a muddle,
How about a little cuddle?

Lana Read (10)
Perry Hall Primary School

SNAKE

I'm green and slithery,
Fat or thin,
I make a hissing sound when I get a fright,
I bite with poison, sharp and tight
And usually come out to hunt at night,
I am scaly and I have a lot of might,
Beware!

Daniel Mayers (11)
Perry Hall Primary School

WILL I GET TO SLEEP?

Boring bed
comfortable too.
The train in the garden keeping
me awake.
I wonder if I will ever
get to sleep tonight?

Christmas in five days
No, no, no, the nights are getting longer.
Will I get to sleep on Christmas Eve?
I wonder if I will ever
get to sleep tonight.

The birds come pecking at the window.
I'm getting colder in this night.
Oh, will I ever get to sleep tonight?

Peter Doorey (10)
Perry Hall Primary School

BALLOONS

Balloons are round, balloons are square,
Balloons are flying everywhere.

Balloons go up, balloons come down,
Balloons are flying round and round.

Balloons are big, balloons are small,
Balloons are very, very tall.

Balloons are bright, balloons are dull,
Balloons are in a festival.

Rachel Holden (11)
Perry Hall Primary School

MY DREAM

I lay on my bed
I could hear the irritating
Sound of the dripping tap
I can hear the whistling
Of the trees outside
The bay windows.
I'm hungry and thirsty but
I'm not getting anywhere
A glimpse of light in
The distance
I can see the patterns
Around my room
Slowly I'm falling into
A world I've never been in before.
I can't see anyone
I've gone into a world of nothing.
I want to go
I wake up to the bright
Streaming light of the sun.

Daniel Pier (9)
Perry Hall Primary School

DRIFTING OFF . . .

The world around me falls into a blur
The brightness of the light slips into darkness,
Dreams make their journey in my mind,
Sleep is chasing and catching me,
Slumber surrounds me now . . .

Michael Rolleston (9)
Perry Hall Primary School

DREAMS

My mum comes in; it's time for bed!
This time is the time that most people dread,
It is good for me cos as it seems
I have the most wonderfully interesting dreams.
Maybe I'll be the King of Wales,
Or in a place where humans have tails,
I could meet a great angel up in Heaven
Or in a place where no one ages past seven.
I like the one where there is an eternal meal
My favourite is when Hogwarts is real.
Another favourite is where I meet Britney Spears,
Or when kids could go out and have a few beers.
A good one is where kids don't go to school
Now that is really cool!
I like all of these because they are all fantastic.
And when I am dreaming them, I get all ecstatic,
I am very proud that these dreams are all mine
I wonder what I'll dream this time?

John McDougall (10)
Poverest Primary School

THE CIRCLE OF LIFE

Life is one big circle,
Throughout life we exchange all we need.
We exchange gases when we breathe.
We convert food into energy and store extra as fat.
Throughout life we exchange knowledge with each other.
We learn from the past and protect our future environment.
We live our lives passing on all our knowledge to the next generation.
This is the meaning of life.

Vicky McGuire (11)
Poverest Primary School

IN THE PARK

A walk in the park
Now what will I see?
There's a dog running fast
Oh! Will it bite me?

I look at the sky
And lay on the grass
And watch all the swans,
As more people pass.

I start to doze off
And dream I'm a cat
Chasing the pigeons
Oh! What was that?

I wake with a jump
Now what was that noise?
Only a football
Kicked by the boys

Over in the playground
I see children play
A wonderful sight
I wish I could stay

But Mum will be worried
If I'm home late
So I'll come again
I just can't wait.

Nichola O'Neill (10)
Poverest Primary School

TWIN SISTERS

Most sisters are annoying,
But mine's among the worst,
Much to my dear mum's dismay,
My sister was born first!

Now we're ten, I sometimes wish,
She'd stop just for a mo,
All the time she chatters,
Listen . . . *I told you so!*

My sister's very pretty,
Of course . . . she looks like me.
She's always after her first date,
But I'm much nicer you see!

She barges into my room . . .
But what she doesn't know
Is that I have my racket,
Poised, ready to throw!

Something I must admit to you . . .
These words are not quite true,
I really love my sister
In spite of all that she can do!

She and I are quite firm friends,
And from our mum we flee!
For she is at her tether's end,
Poor mum . . . bought one, got one free!

Rebecca Mattacks (10)
Poverest Primary School

ANIMALS

I like animals big or small
I like animals short or tall
I like animals wild or tame
The zebra's stripes, the lion's mane

They live their lives, wild and free
Some on land, some on the sea
Some have feathers and wings to fly
They soar above us in the sky

They hunt their prey come what may
So they can survive another day
Watching, waiting, lying low
Stalking their kill and off they go

I like animals smooth or rough
I like animals weak or tough
I like animals fierce or kind
I like animals of every kind.

Andrew Darby (9)
Poverest Primary School

THE GORILLA

G   is for grumpy when disturbed by others
O   is for observing the world around him,
R   is for a relative of man
I   is for insects, a favourite food
L   is for leafy areas, where you will find him sitting
L   is for leather on his face, feet and hands,
A   is for ape, he is larger than man.

Benedict Leonard (9)
Poverest Primary School

A BOAT DRIFTING AWAY FROM A DISTANT PAST

In the far away mist
Of the night that sneaks up
The water crashes against the rocks
And all I can do is just stare and watch

As my heart starts to race
The boat draws near
And the sea whisks away
And the cries of terror are all I can hear

And then the boat is eaten
By the sea's hunger
And what once sailed there
Sails no longer.

Cassey Gaywood (11)
Poverest Primary School

A DAY IN WINTER

'It's cold outside.'
The weatherman said
just as we were going to bed.
When we get up
it could be snowing.
We'll go outside
our noses will be glowing.
Fingers and toes feel like they've
stopped growing.
We'll wrap up warm
and run down the lane
and if it gets colder
run home again.

Sophie Pritchard (9)
Poverest Primary School

I WISH . . .

I wish I didn't have to do this
I told you before I'm no good.
Poetry isn't easy for me
These words just about rhyme as they should.

I wish I could go and play football,
I don't feel the cold you know.
Instead I'm stuck in my bedroom,
Writing poems, and looking out of the window.

I wish we could win the lottery.
Imagine what it would be like.
I'd buy all the computer games ever made,
And a mobile, and a scooter and a bike.

But here I am writing my poem,
Mum won't let me go out till I'm through.
So here's one about all my wishes
And hope they all come true!

Jack Fawcett (11)
Poverest Primary School

LAND OF VAST ANNOYMENT

A vast planet called Earth
Is where I had my birth.
I was born a maker of sin
I should have gone in the baby bin.

Helped by a touch of magic I had
Mum was not in the least bit sad.
I now call Earth the land of vast annoyment
Everyone knows how to annoy me,
It must be a special ointment.

My parents blinded with adoration
Find seeing me a great sensation.
And now it has been written
I'm about to torture that lovely kitten.

James Cresswell (11)
Poverest Primary School

THE LITTLE MONSTER

The little monster isn't what you expect
It is my little brother,
He really is a terror.

If you see him (well hear him)
You will know what he's like
Please give pity on us for he lives with us!

If I get something new
He throws himself upon the floor
Screaming 'You never loved me!'

Until a little old dear comes over with a lolly
He really is the spoilt one
For this is the way he acts,

'Buy my toys and get my sweets,
Or else I'll tell my granny!'
For Granny gives him what he wants.

You can see what I mean now!
Would you please come and take him away
Before we lose our minds!

Lorraine Hough (11)
Poverest Primary School

REMEMBER

My type of day
Would be in the USA
The sun, the trees
I'm being spoilt but, hey!

Another good day
Would be in France
We would run around
And sing and dance.

But what we have to remember,
Is the little kids who can't have fun
As we remember all the memories
And everything we have done.

Thomas Whelan (11)
Poverest Primary School

ODE TO DOUGHNUTS

Doughnuts are sticky, a pleasure to eat,
Leaving sugar on your lips and
Jam on your teeth.
Warm and fresh,
Straight from the baker's, or from Tesco's,
Reduced 20p or under.

Doughnuts for breakfast, doughnuts for tea,
Doughnuts with custard and doughnuts with cream.
For different people there's
Jam or custard, for instance some
People prefer them with mustard.

But I myself prefer them plain, for I do
Not want large weight gain!
Shall I choose doughnuts big or doughnuts small?
Well, retrieve some now and
I'll eat them all!

Megan-Rose Lightwing (10)
Poverest Primary School

THE SEASONS

There is not a season in the year
that does not bring me a little cheer.
The seasons come, the seasons go,
and as they do I find I grow.

Spring comes first, bursting with life,
as the creatures begin hunting a wife.
Every bud starts to poke out its shoots,
and I find I've grown out of my boots.

Summertime brings the heat and sun,
the season that enjoys laughter and fun.
Everywhere looks and smells so sweet,
and I play football till dusk as a treat.

Autumn brings changes to all the trees,
leaves begin tumbling in the breeze.
Bonfires are built with the greatest of care,
and I make a bonfire as part of a dare.

Winter brings the cold and the dark,
snow covers everything in the park.
Everywhere is covered in decorations,
and I enjoy the Christmas celebrations.

Michael McGuire (9)
Poverest Primary School

THE FUTURE

Spice Girls and scooters
Flying rockets and planes
Mobiles and laptop computers
Will soon be a thing of the past

Generations to come
Will think of these things, old and useless
But, just maybe, to some
They will be pleasant memories of the past

So what now, this new twenty-first century
Where will we go? What will we see?
Flying skateboards, hopefully there will be plenty
To whisk us off on holiday
To Jupiter, Saturn and maybe Mars and the moon.

Grace Gaywood (9)
Poverest Primary School

THE MOON AND THE SUN

The moon is light
Because of the sun so bright
The moon is so far away
So you won't get to it in a day

The sun is a fiery orange ball,
It brings daylight to us all,
It shines on the Earth as it turns,
But you have to be careful in case it burns.

Steven Cresswell (9)
Poverest Primary School

MY BABY BROTHER

I have a baby brother
He is very sweet
He is nearly standing
On his own two feet.

My baby brother
Has a lot of toys
All day long he makes
Lots of noise.

I give him baths
And change his nappy
I'll do anything
To keep him happy.

And finally when he's in bed
'At last I can get some rest' to
myself I said.

Lauren Sweetlove (10)
Poverest Primary School

RAIN

The rain against my window,
Woke me up one day.
I was very disappointed,
I could not go out to play
So instead I had my friends round
They all stayed for tea.
The rain had stopped, the sun came out,
And it was only half-past three.

Sianna Louise Grover (9)
Poverest Primary School

I WISH...

I wish that everything could be right
Shops are never burgled
People in the street never fight
I wish that peace would rule.

I wish that wars would not break out
People walk hand in hand
And with joy, not anger, would shout
I wish that peace would rule.

I wish that children in the street
Could play safely with friends,
Not worrying who they meet
I wish that peace would rule.

I wish for families to love each other
And the whole world would unite.
Like a sister and her brother
I wish that peace would rule.

Samuel Hanson (10)
Poverest Primary School

IF I HAD A HAMSTER

If I had a hamster
I think I'd call him Harry
Then I'd get a female one
So that they could marry.

Harry and his wife might find,
It's lonely being two of a kind.
They might decide to have some more
Three baby hamsters or maybe four.

I'd care for them each and every day,
I'd feed them and then we'd play.
I'd let them run about their house,
Then I might get a mouse.

If I had a mouse,
I think I'd call him Sammy.
Then I'd get a female one
And so that they could be married . . .

Cathy Alcoran (10)
Poverest Primary School

STARS

I see a star in the sky
One appearing all the time,
I don't know why they are so high
Oh I wish I could fly.

I try and try to fly up high
To touch the stars that go by;
I jump off this
I jump off that
But my feet keep landing flat.

I tie balloons upon my back
But my body must be flat;
I try and try
To fly up high,
To reach the stars
That go by . . .

Jade Young (11)
Poverest Primary School

CHILD ABUSE

Don't hit that little girl
Don't hit her in her stomach
Don't hit her on her head
She might just fall down dead.

Don't tie her in a corner
Don't lock her in a box
Don't call her nasty names
Give her back her favourite socks.

Don't punish or punch or burn her
Don't strip her of her pride
Because you're in a bad mood.

Treat your child with kindness
Treat her with respect
Treat her like a precious jewel
Help her intellect.

If you're getting beaten
If you're getting punched
If you've had no breakfast, dinner or lunch.

He could go to prison
He could get a fine
He might even get abused
He'll have to stay in line.

So tell it to your teacher
Tell it to your friend
Tell it to 'Childline' and
Bring it to an end.

Rosie Yates (10)
Raglan Primary School

THE INDIAN EARTHQUAKE

The ground shook like a rumble of thunder,
Land fell apart as quick as a wink,
People's screams became louder and more terrified by the second.

The sky grew as black as a bumblebee's back
Buildings collapsed like a crumbled biscuit,
More people got buried by the minute.

The earthquake has stopped so suddenly,
Only moans of such pain could be heard,
A lot of people we have lost, forever.

Kate Giannini (9)
Raglan Primary School

ANIMALS

Snails, snakes and slugs slither on the ground
Snails have shells
And
Snakes have tails

Tortoises are slow
Cheetahs are fast

Birds fly high in the sky
    While
Cats and dogs walk on the ground

Fish swim in the sea
Birds fly in the sky
    And
Cats, dogs, elephants, monkeys, hippos, rhinos, wolves, foxes, rabbits
Bears, gorillas, squirrels, rats, mice and apes
Live on land.

Beverley Agyeman (9)
Rangefield Primary School

CLAIRE'S HAIR

There was a little girl called Claire
She went to school without her hair
Her hair kept growing and growing and growing
This happened without Claire knowing.

As she got home and saw her hair
She cried and cried in despair
She tried her mum, her mum wasn't in
She tried to throw it in the bin.

Her hair came alive and jumped on her head
She fainted and looked as if she was dead
Her hair got evil and jumped through the door
And landed smack right on the floor.

Her mum came in and saw her bald
'What has happened to you, you fool'
Her mum smacked her on the butt
Then the pair walked in with Pizza Hut.

Jamie Muller (10)
Rangefield Primary School

THE HEART THAT STOLE VALENTINE'S DAY

The heart that stole Valentine's Day
Was very gentle
He found a very nice girlfriend called Valentine
He shot Valentine with his heart arrow and they fell in love
Valentine's heart was pumping very fast
And they made a lovely couple in love
They were very happy
And went everywhere, firing heart arrows at quiet couples
They lived happily ever after.

Robert Allen (8)
Rangefield Primary School

SPAGHETTI BOLOGNAISE

It's long and thin
And stringy too

And sometimes comes
With meat balls, whoo-hoo!

If it does
Then down it goes
Down my tummy to my toes.

Down my throat to my gut
Then a bit of wind comes out my butt.

Up it comes in one big gulp
Down the toilet all the pulp.

Then I get a tummy ache
Oh, will I need a wake?

Natasha Wilkinson (10)
Rangefield Primary School

THE DOG

The dog walked through the fog
A log got in the way
The dog went in a house
He saw a ghost, the dog said 'Ggghhost!'
But the dog was brave, he bashed the ghost up
An army of dragons came running down the stairs
He gave the dragons some drugs to make them all dopey
He had some ice cream to make him strong
He went upstairs to get special powers
He found them!

Liam Dorta-Martin (9)
Rangefield Primary School

The Witch's Kitchen

The smoked-filled room
Full of cauldrons bubbling
Frogs hopping all over the place
And the faint smell of garlic.

I could feel the warmth of the cauldrons
An old wooden box
Full of big cookery books
With gruesome recipes inside.

A lot of dust from a dreary cupboard
Which held within it
Things too horrible
And unpleasant to explain.

A small witch's cat hissing in the corner
As black as night
And eyes like car headlights
Coming down a dark road.

In the fridge
There is a smell of sour milk
A bunch of rotten vegetables
And some assorted eyeballs.

In the cupboards
There are some mice
And some bloody body bits
There are also vast amounts of potion bottles.

Thomas Allen (11)
Rangefield Primary School

THE WRITER OF THIS POEM

The writer of this poem
Is as funny as a clown,
As sharp as a razor,
As greedy as a hippo.

As clever as a cat,
As angry as the colour red,
As lazy as an unmade bed,
As clean as a doctor's hands.

As focused as a lion on his prey,
As smooth as a desk top,
As keen as mustard,
As good as gold.

Anders Wickham (11)
Rangefield Primary School

MY TEACHER

My teacher is tall and very slim
She has a friend who is very trim

She has green hair
And she is very fair

She calls us pests
Just like all the rest
And gives us loads of tests

We love her though
We hope she'll grow
And all she ever does is groan
When she's on the telephone.

Stacey Rogers (10)
Rangefield Primary School

CHOCOLATE

Chocolate is the best
It's better than all the rest
I could eat it every day
And never give it all away.

I've never tasted anything better
It doesn't taste anything like pepper
It tastes so sweet
It's better than smelly feet.

I'm a big chocolate fan
And I've got a dark chocolate tan
I like to eat chocolate and I always will
I like to eat chocolate and it will never make me ill.

Amy Hayden (10)
Rangefield Primary School

EDD

I know a boy called Edd
He liked to stand on his head
In his bed
He would sleep
This boy called Edd

Edd, Edd, Edd
That boy called Edd
One day he was standing on his head
When *crash* went Edd
With his head.

Lucy Bick (8)
Rangefield Primary School

THE GOBLIN'S CELLAR

The goblin's dark and dingy cellar,
Is full of unicorns' and dwarves' bones.
It smells like rotten eggs and decaying fish.
If you think that's diabolical you should see the bedroom.

The goblin's nasty, stinky bedroom
Is covered in mud and blood from warm spaghetti.
It feels like there are maggots under your feet.
If you think that's ghastly you should see the kitchen.

In the goblin's dusty kitchen,
The creaking oven is crackling.
The air tastes like mouldy socks.
Do you know what I smell . . .
Cooked humans!

Brett Dowling-Jones (11)
Rangefield Primary School

ALIEN SPACECRAFT

In my bed I'm fast asleep
Not so fast, I cannot peep
I see a light through my window bright
Stars are not the only thing in the sky tonight
An alien spacecraft takes its flight
At my bedroom window tonight, the spacecraft hoovered
Shall I be bothered to look out my window?
The door opens, the smoke clears then I wake up and make up my mind
I look out the window and find it's gone
It's all a dream, my alien spaceship was not what it seemed.

Taylor Wallace (9)
Rangefield Primary School

SCHOOL

Boring old school again
I bet you it's going to rain
Noisy class, same old work
Maths, English, oops I burped
We go out to play at quarter-past ten
I played 'Lion In The Den'
Time for assembly
I sat next to Beverley
On it went, I wish it was lunch
Oh, what's on the menu, I hope it will crunch
Went back to class, did science and art
I had a look who was next on the chart
Time to go home, I'm sitting on the floor
I'm going to play my Nintendo 64.

Kelly Foxcroft (11)
Rangefield Primary School

THE GOBLIN'S CELLAR

The goblin's cellar is slimy and full of cobwebs
Glasses filled to the rim with thick dust in which he kept
Frogs' eyes, dragons' tongues, pigs' guts and lizards' toes

You can hear him making potions, bang, bang, bang!
You can smell a musky, eggy smell (yuck)
And you can hear his cruel laugh, cackling - ha, ha, ha!

You feel scared but you're not, it's just the way it looks
Your nerves are shaking
But you don't know who you're going to meet . . . next!

Brogan Green (11)
Rangefield Primary School

THE WITCH'S KITCHEN

The rusty aroma of lavender from a flaming stick
The cauldron bubbling, in it a potion made
A leaking tap, bent up and rusty
It has made a puddle on the floor
From this, weeds are growing
The brown painted cupboards swinging open and closed
Showing many multicoloured potions
Some deadly, some harmless
Her skinny black cat asleep in a pile of worn-out rags
The black walls are covered in cracks
From the cracks, mould is growing
The tiny smashed up window, dusty and covered in cobwebs
That haven't felt fresh air for years
The witch's ancient broomstick thrown carelessly into a corner
is falling apart
But as you look at this dark and dingy kitchen
You suddenly see her shiny cabinet, one of the best in the world
Clean, sparkling, expensive and brand new
Who knows what's in there.

Sophie Savage (11)
Rangefield Primary School

THE BROKEN HEART AT VALENTINE'S

One Valentine's I saw a broken heart
It said to me I'm alone at this part
It said hello in soppy tears and ran back home
I saw his ex-girlfriend walking down the road
I said go home to your ex-boyfriend
It's now Valentine's Day, don't break his heart anymore.

Charlotte Wingfield (9)
Rangefield Primary School

THE WITCH'S KITCHEN

The witch's kitchen is haunted with dead things
They move in the night, creeping around
Trying to eat the un-living creatures
The witch's kitchen makes me feel creepy
Because someone, somewhere is underneath the floorboards
The witch's kitchen is full of dead bodies
The floor is slippery and is full of blood.

I see a suspicious spider looking with his angry eyes
Because he did not get the creature he wanted
He was also angry because he only had two legs
Because the nasty, wicked witch had taken them off
with her high heel shoes.

The witch's kitchen is gigantic
You might even get lost
The witch is waiting for more lost people
So she can put their bones in the cauldron for her dinner.

Jennifer Forde (10)
Rangefield Primary School

THE WITCH'S KITCHEN

The witch's kitchen all tattered and torn
The crimson cupboards hanging on the rusty, worn out hooks
The burning smell of deadly scent from the black, bubbling cauldron.

The smell of flaming acid flowing around in the small cramped kitchen
From the glass jars of toads' legs and many more disgusting things
Comes a sickening smell
Which makes me feel weak at the knees.

Bonita Brindle (11)
Rangefield Primary School

THE INVENTOR'S WORKSHOP

The inventor's workshop smells of scrap metal
His white cloak is now grey from years of dust
The machines are glowing from the rays of the sun
The light is glimmering where it's been left out
The shelves are full of bits of pieces and chemicals
with dead flies and spiders
His hands are very competent and he can still hear the banging
and churning of the machines
When he goes into the laboratory he remembers
when he was an inventor
I think he was a great inventor but that's not what he thinks
His glasses are black from the blast of the chemicals
He stopped inventing because he got too old.

Micheala Virgo (11)
Rangefield Primary School

THE DOG

The hairy dog jumped over a log but couldn't see in the fog
The big, hairy, frightened dog managed to escape from the fog
He sees the most beautiful puppy he had ever seen
He barks and looks at the puppy and starts running to the puppy
The big, hairy dog falls asleep on the grass
Next morning the fluffy, big, hairy dog went to find the cute
little puppy
The cute puppy was gone, the hairy dog barked
The dog jumped over the fence
And saw the cute, sleepy puppy sleeping.

Anusha Badal (8)
Rangefield Primary School

IT WAS NOT ME

It was not me
So let me be

He did it Miss
He used his fist

Check it if you don't believe me
Ask gooey Louie Lee

I did not punch Kelly
I did not punch her in the belly

I do not believe you John
I think a little too far you have gone

How I'm getting the blame
That really is a shame

It's not very fair
She pulled me off my chair

When I go home and tell my mum
I hope she does not smack my bum.

Kayla Patricia Dawkins (11)
Rangefield Primary School

A SMUGGLER'S LIFE

The smuggler's cave is full of treasure,
A smuggler's life is a life of pleasure,
Gold and silver glisten in the sun,
They grab things quick and then they run.

They wear all sorts of things they steal,
Of silky clothes from head to heal,
They pick-pocket with a smile on their face,
They leave the scene without a trace.

The shops are empty, the people gone,
This is a great time for some,
They just break in, take what they please,
And leave without paying the fees.

They creep back home to the cave,
And in the sea they wash and bathe,
They sit and think what to stand,
I wonder how they really feel.

Lucy Toomey (11)
Rangefield Primary School

CHRISTMAS

One snowy Christmas
When I went out to play
I saw all the snow
People were shouting in Downham way

It was very windy
The snow was falling down
Snowmen in the garden
Snow all around

Presents to open
Under the tree
Some for my family
And some for me

Turkey for dinner
Brussels sprouts
Having fun in the evening
That's what Christmas is all about.

Samantha Gleeson (10)
Rangefield Primary School

The Witch's Kitchen

The explosive potions are full of poets
Who are dead and have been dug up
Why not leave them in the spirit of the dead
'Because I want to make bloodsucking potions,' cackled the witch
'The poets make it more mouth-watering because of their tasty words
They are so bloodsucking for me
When they are cooked I eat them hungrily.

When I am eating, I feel rhymes in my mouth
This is because the poet is still alive in my mouth
Reading hungry poems
Then I swallow him and he is dead.

Michael Dorey (11)
Rangefield Primary School

Nature

Butterflies fluttering on a flower
While the dragonfly's flying with all its power
All the ants are lifting stones
While the bumblebees are making honeycombs
In the field were growing crops
While a big, green grasshopper leaps and hops
Soon the sun sets
It's the end of the day
All the animals begin to scurry away
The birds are flying in the sky
Are the clouds about to cry?

Aisha Derbel (11)
Rangefield Primary School

SWEETS ARE NICE

Sweets are nice
We kids eat them every day
Even adults can't resist them
Every day we chew and chew
Though we brush our teeth each day
Sweets make them rot away

Adults tell you sweets aren't real
Really Mum I can't resist
Even you know they exist

Nephews and nieces ask for sweets
I say 'You're too young so go to sleep.'
'Can I have chocolate then?'
'Even you know chocolate is a sweet.'

Thomas Hogg (10)
Rangefield Primary School

LIFE

Life is full of ups and downs
It's full of happy faces and frowns
Life is in every creature, country and town
What about when you're down?
Life seems so dull and brown
But when you're happy with a bright face
Life is full of rejoice and grace
So when you have your happy face
Just remember you can fill the world
With rejoice and grace.

Bethany Rooks (9)
Rangefield Primary School

LOONEY TOONS POEM

Bugs Bunny, he is so funny
He is such a cool bunny

Daffy Duck is a cool duck
He always steps in muck

Road Runner is very fast
Wile E Coyote is always last

Taz has big, sharp teeth
Even though he doesn't eat beef

Sylvester always chases Tweety
But I think Tweety is a little sweety

Tweety is a cute bird
He looks like lemon curd

Elmer Thud always carries a gun
His sportsmanship is a lot of fun.

Daniel Reeves (10)
Rangefield Primary School

THE CLOWN

The circus clown came to town,
His great big boots stamped up and down,
His face was painted red and white,
His nose was red and shining bright.

He rolls and tumbles round the ring,
His big, black car is a funny thing,
He drives it round and round and round,
The doors, the roof, the wheels fall off,
There's so much smoke, it makes us cough.

He is a very jolly clown,
He makes us laugh and never frown,
He throws water everywhere,
But because we're happy, we don't care.

Aylin Unlu (10)
Rangefield Primary School

DUDLEY

A fluffy puppy, he started off,
All cute and cuddly and soft.
With eyes of brown and a black, wet nose,
When I took his picture he used to pose.

His tail, though just a little stump,
Wagged so much, it used to thump!
When the postman came he ran to the hall,
To get the letters with an almighty pull.

For bickies and chocs he used to jump,
He really was a little lump.
He loved to play and fetch his ball,
And just ignored me when I did call.

When growing old he still did play,
But in his bed he used to stay.
His 'forty winks' turned into days,
When I shouted 'Walkies!' he'd say 'No way!'

He had the sweetest floppy ears,
I loved him so for many years.

Leia Thomas (10)
Rangefield Primary School

CRISPS

Crisps crunch when you munch them
When you step on them they crackle
They come in different flavours
They are very, very tasty
I can't live without them
I have to have at least three packets a day
My favourite flavour is prawn cocktail
Actually I have lots of favourites.

Cilem Karabeyaz (11)
Rangefield Primary School

STAR

A star comes out at night
It shines so bright
A star brightens up the sky
It shows me where to go at night
It glitters and glows.

Rebecca Collins (8)
Seal CE Primary School

STAR

A star shoots in the sky
A star glitters at night
A star shines like silver
A star is so bright
You can make a wish.

Martin Roff (7)
Seal CE Primary School

WHAT IS GREEN?

Green is the grass waving around
Green are the leaves flowing off the trees
Green is a field so lovely and bright
Green is a caterpillar squiggling around
Green is a tree waving left and right
Green is a ball bouncing up and down
Green is a traffic light that says 'Go!'
Green is a mountain so high and without any snow.

Amanda McGinniss (9)
Seal CE Primary School

DOLPHINS

Dolphins splash all day long looking for fish
They have two fins like flippers
Skin so silky
Eyes so bright like the stars
A face so friendly smiling at you
Dolphins have lots of tricks.

Stephanie Coppins (8)
Seal CE Primary School

THE SNAKE

It slides over pebbles, rocks and grass
It hisses at its prey first
Then stings it with its tail
Then its prey is paralysed
After that it eats it in one gulp!

Anthony Stewart (8)
Seal CE Primary School

WHAT IS BLUE?

Blue is in a rainbow of lovely colours
Blue is a whale flapping its tail
Blue is water flooding the house
Blue is a puddle splashing around
Blue is a dolphin flapping its flippers
Blue is rain falling from the sky
Blue is the sky, cloudy at night
Blue are tears dropping from eyes
Blue is a jumper that you wear to school
Blue is a blue tit singing its song
Blue are bluebells, lovely and frail.

Lee Roberts (8)
Seal CE Primary School

WHAT IS BLUE?

Blue is the sea, waving in the night,
Blue is a dolphin shiny and bright,
Blue are eyes filling with fright,
Blue is a river flowing and bitter,
Blue is the sky when the clouds have gone,
Blue is a blue tit singing its song,
Blue are the bluebells lovely and frail,
Blue is a whale flapping its tail.

Chloe Checkley (7)
Seal CE Primary School

WHAT IS RED?

Red is a fire engine saving people's lives.
Red is a tongue slobbering and wet.
Red are lips bright and rosy-red.
Red is the colour of a devil's anger.
Red is the colour of juicy strawberries.
Red is the colour of blood dripping.
Red is the colour of autumn leaves.
Red is a heart beating so fast.
Red is a firework shooting with a *blast!*
Red is the sun bulging with heat.
Red is the colour of a stop sign on the street.

Scott Nowers (7)
Seal CE Primary School

WHAT IS RED?

Red is blood dripping from my arm
Red is a robin feeding its chicks
Red is an apple delicious and yummy
Red are the lips moving around
Red is a crab pinching my nose
Red is a toadstool covering a mouse
Red are leaves in autumn
Red is the sun blazing on the sea.

Jade King (8)
Seal CE Primary School

WHAT IS BLUE?

Blue is the sky, lovely and bright
Blue is the ocean waving at night
Blue is a dolphin swimming in the sea
Blue is the colour of people's eyes
Blue is the water dripping from the tap
Blue is a blue tit singing its song
Blue is a whale's tail flapping along.

Lily Rose (9)
Seal CE Primary School

WHAT IS BLACK?

Black is the sky at night, shining and bright
Black is the blackboard, dark and horrible
Black is a gorilla, big and hairy
Black is the mud, sticky and gooey
Black are plimsolls, warm and cosy
Black is a monkey, nice and snuggly.

Gemma Scott (8)
Seal CE Primary School

I LIKE THE FEEL OF THINGS

I like the feel of my bed
when I sleep in it.

I like the feel of my teddy
when I cuddle her.

I like the feel of smoothness
of my silky dress.

I like the feel of the air
when I smoothly slither across the classroom.

I like the feel of my hair
when I brush it.

Heidi Jessop (7)
Seal CE Primary School

WHAT IS BLUE?

Blue is a whale, flapping its tail.
Blue is the sea, glittering at night.
Blue is an eye, staring at you.
Blue are bluebells when you go to a forest.
Blue are dolphins when they do tricks.
Blue is a blueberry juicy and sweet.
Blue is the sky going by.
Blue is the pond where ducks swim.

Tamanna Miah (7)
Seal CE Primary School

CHRISTMAS FOR ME

Christmas for me is decorations and snow.
Christmas for me is roast and wine.
Christmas for me is Christmas carols.
Christmas for me is tasting the roast dinner.
Christmas for me is feeling the Christmas paper.
Christmas for me is all the presents.
Christmas for me is seeing my family on Christmas Day.
Christmas for me is seeing all the presents around the tree.

Sophie Primett (9)
Seal CE Primary School

WHAT IS GOLD?

Gold are the lovely stars at night, shiny and bright,
Gold is the Christmas robin, singing to you at night,
Gold is the tinsel tickling you when it touches you,
Gold is flashing in your eyes,
Gold is jumping in your heart,
Gold is the shiny glitter, twinkling in your eyes,
Gold is the Christmas angel flying around at night,
Gold is a precious ring when someone goes to a wedding,
Gold is a shiny watch, brand new when it comes to you.

Tanya Waghorn (7)
Seal CE Primary School

WHAT IS RED?

Red is the sun, bright and shiny,
Red is a crab, snappy and prickly,
Red are flames, burning to ash,
Red is blood, when you get a gash,
Red are bricks that you construct for a house,
Red is a toadstool, sheltering a mouse,
Red are roses, colourful in the field,
Red is the colour of a battle shield.

Samuel Kettle (8)
Seal CE Primary School

WHAT IS BLUE?

Blue is the sky, lovely and bright,
Blue is the sea, shiny and nice,
Blue are the raindrops, splitting and splatting,
Blue are the doors, silvery and shimmery,
Blue are the books, glittery and silvery,
Blue is the paper, loud and crackly,
Blue is the weaving in and out,
Blue are the leaves, in and out of autumn,
Blue are the jumpers on the children,
Blue are the spellings, checking if they are right.

Zoe Dunmill (7)
Seal CE Primary School

CHRISTMAS FOR ME

Christmas for me is decorations and snow,
Christmas for me is the taste of sweets and roast dinner,
Christmas for me is the sound of snow on the window
                                    and the sound of bells,
Christmas for me is the smell of pudding and holly,
Christmas for me is the softness of snow and the spiky pine needles,
But the most important thing about Christmas for me is seeing my
                                    grandma and grandad.

Jacob Lowe (7)
Seal CE Primary School

WHAT IS RED?

Red is the colour of a crab,
Sharp and spiky, dark at night.
Red is the colour of fire,
Mighty and light.
Red is the colour of blood,
Dark and runny down your body.
Red is the colour of a brick,
Solid and thick.

Adam Orme (8)
Seal CE Primary School

RAP CAT ON THE MAT

I'm a cat on the mat,
Just by the door,
Yeah, my owner's not rich,
Yeah, my owner's not poor.

I'm lean,
I'm mean,
I'm a
fighting machine.

If you're a rat or a mouse
and you're in my house,
be cautious, beware,
you're in for a scare.

If you want to be bashed,
bruised and constantly beaten,
come to my house,
you might get eaten.

Jonathan Stowell (10)
Sevenoaks Prep School

VOYAGE IN SPACE

I wonder what it's like to be in space.
Are the stars bright?
Do they only shine at night?

Is there life on Mars?
Do they drive cars?
And would they drink in bars?

I would like to travel through the galaxy
With Captain Kirk on the Starship Enterprise,
Or maybe I could go on Apollo 13
And help them to get home safely.

If I went on holiday to a planet,
I wonder what I would do.
Could I go swimming?
And if I did, would the water stay in the pool,
Or would it float out, if there was no gravity?
When I dived into the pool, would I float into space?
Where would we go for dinner?
A restaurant?
But would there be one?
If we went to McDonald's we could use the drive-thru!
Would I make any friends?
It would be great to meet ET
We could ride our flying bikes through the air,
Exploring craters everywhere.
Travelling through time,
That would seem strange to me.
I'd see all those things and be back in time for tea,
Maybe.
One day we'll see!

Antony Grant (10)
Sevenoaks Prep School

THE ALIEN

They live in space,
they run with pace.
They're green,
but not easily seen.

They have 18 legs
and 18 ears,
but their peers
have 25 ears and 28 years.

They lived in the Med,
and they were well fed
and every year they grew a new head.

They had a boat,
that was normally afloat.
They came to Earth,
they landed in Perth
and the first thing they saw was turf.

They felt very black,
'cause they went back
to the planet Firlamaback.

Josh Perry (11)
Sevenoaks Prep School

SWITCHED ON

A computer had a problem,
It couldn't be switched on.
All its life it sat on a desk,
Always having a rest.

An electrician came,
And fixed the frame,
But he forgot about the switch.

After it was fixed,
It was always being played with,
And the computer loved it,
But then it couldn't be switched off.

Sam Hull (10)
Sevenoaks Prep School

ALIENS

Out of space
is their base

In space they
have no pace

They have four eyes
and only eat pies

They are green
and not normally seen

They have twelve toes
and one nose

They have two million teeth
for eating corned beef

They have three heads
and they wet their beds

They all have five hands
and they are all in bands

Some people think they live in the sea
and one of them is me!

Sam Cox (11)
Sevenoaks Prep School

ALIENS

They fly through the air,
Without any care.

They have seven eyes,
And they only eat flies.

When they see Earth,
They want to attack,
But they can't,
'Cause they can't stand on turf.

They live on the moon,
And we will know very soon,
If they live on the planet called Mars.

And with the Hubble telescope,
They haven't a hope,
Of hiding out there forever!

Oliver Parrett (11)
Sevenoaks Prep School

THE FIRST PIRATES

47 pirates,
Floating on the sea,
Heading to America,
To find the Golden Key,
Landing on the shore,
They kissed the ground beneath them,
Soon realizing that the natives were to eat them!

Hayley Kramer (11)
Sevenoaks Prep School

VOYAGE

Race loser
    Space cruiser
        Speed bruiser
            Bike rider
            Mountain climber
    Swim diver
Car driver
    Rocket soarer
        Ship tourer
            Alien ship
            Very quick
    Fast train
Wide lane
    Speed gain
        Over drain
            Slow down

Put brake down!

Alex Barnett (10)
Sevenoaks Prep School

VOYAGE

Rocket soarer
    Ship tourer
        Car driver
            Swim diver
        Train traveller
    Pilot scavenger
        Truck tower
            Boat rower.

Tom Boardman (10)
Sevenoaks Prep School

SWIMMING WITH DOLPHINS

Swimming with dolphins was such a surprise,
I could hardly believe my eyes,
They were so beautiful, so sleek, so thin,
With one arm round its dorsal fin,
I glided across the freezing Atlantic,
My friends around me were going frantic.

For half an hour my life was unbeatable,
The excitement I was feeling was unbelievable,
Because I love animals, I couldn't resist,
So I fed them with some little fish,
When I got out the air was so warm,
But I wanted to go back to the new baby born,
When I was changing I realized I knew,
I wish I was a dolphin too.

Hannah Berry (11)
Sevenoaks Prep School

MY DAD

He's older than me but has less hair
When I need him he's always there
He likes to travel and take his time
He makes me feel special and he's kind
He's hardworking and fun to be with
He likes computer games and finishes in a jiff
He makes me feel happy when I'm down
He's tall and smart and makes me feel proud
When I am old and not so thin
I hope that I am just like him.

Michael Hobern (10)
Sevenoaks Prep School

TV Programmes

Jonathan Creek is a mystery,
The Simpsons make me laugh,
Some things I can't get my head round,
And some shows are just plain daft.

Recess, an American cartoon show,
With TJ, the head of a gang,
Randal snitches on everyone,
Miss Finster yells with a bang.

Dad watches sport and the market update,
We all think it's a bore,
He also watches the football show,
To get the latest score.

I always watch TV,
It really is lots of fun,
But Mum won't let me watch it,
Until my prep is done.

Stuart Bennett (10)
Sevenoaks Prep School

The River

The river sways down an angry waterfall,
Foam spurts up as the river
Crashes into the water beneath.
Animals on the riverbank drink,
Feeling the chill of the water
As it flows through their throats.

Alexander Blanning (10)
Sevenoaks Prep School

UNTITLED

One day I went on a roller coaster,
My brain was rattling like a toaster.
When I got on I was scared,
I looked at the top then I stared.
When we started to go, I closed my eyes,
Because, of course, I was afraid of heights.
I opened my eyes thinking we were back,
But we were only at the top, so I said 'Oh drat!'
We went through a maze of big hills
And I thought to myself should I start taking pills?
At the end of the ride I thought it was fun,
And I said, 'Please can I go on again Mum?'

Sean Higginson (10)
Sevenoaks Prep School

CATS IN THE NIGHT

Cats in the night get out of sight,
'Cause they're in for a fight,
To show all their might in the fight
To impress the ladies in sight
With eyes shining bright,
For the young ones around
Learning for when it's their turn
Lots of cats on the tiles,
They will walk for miles,
In the morning they return.

Daniel Conway (10)
Sevenoaks Prep School

THE CACKLE PARTY

It's Hallowe'en at last
We can spook again
People who are sleeping
Tuck your heads back in

Because we are witches
We can see you anywhere you go
Oh
We can see you anywhere you go

Under the covers
Under the bed
In the closet
Or in your head

It doesn't matter where you try to hide
We are witches and have the power
To search for you until the daylight hour

To spook you, to spook you, to spook you
Ha ha ha ha ha.

Tabitha Lee-Stephens (9)
St James' CE Junior School, Tunbridge Wells

NICOLA

Nicola is a clock with its hands whizzing around
She is the middle of the day when the sun is shining
She is a fresh, juicy apple that has always got enough to give
And a red, warm and friendly colour
Like the powerful wind that won't stop blowing
Like a cheeky, energetic monkey swinging from vine to vine.

Alice Halliday (9)
St James' CE Junior School, Tunbridge Wells

A DAY AT THE SEASIDE

I cannot wait till after school,
I'm going to the beach to get cool,
I've been thinking about it all day,
I can't wait to go and play.

I looked out the window to see the beach,
Then I turned round and saw someone eating a peach.
I opened the door excitedly,
Then Mum said, 'Who can't wait to get to the sea?'

The sand was slipping through my toes,
The sun was shining on my nose.
I long to jump into the sea,
But Mum said I've got to have my tea.

It was the time to go and swim
And then I said, 'Look, there's Kim.'
We played and played in the sun
And then we bought a sticky bun.

In an hour it was time to go,
I walked out of the sea very slow.
I wish I could come another day,
To have more time to stay and play.

Sophie Rance (8)
St James' CE Junior School, Tunbridge Wells

TIME

T   he flash of cold, shiny steel
I   roam the desolate fields
M sword I need no longer
E   vening wind will carry my spirit home.

Michael Marshall (10)
St James' CE Junior School, Tunbridge Wells

PLAYTIME

Balls flying through the air
Children running everywhere
Clapping
Laughing
Not a care
Screaming
Shouting
No time to spare

Shoes scuffing
Trousers ripping
Happy playing
Fun for all

The bell tolls with a chime
Worn out children form a line
Playtime is over
It's learning time!

Joseph Nagle (10)
St James' CE Junior School, Tunbridge Wells

FAIRIES

Fairies crowded with bumblebees,
Fairies crowded with magic keys.
They flew so high in the sky so clear,
People found it hard to hear.
Fairies crowded round people's teeth
And wrapped them round the leaf.
They always, always come at night,
Never in the light.

Lauren Pomfret (7)
St James' CE Junior School, Tunbridge Wells

ASHLEY

Ashley is a TV, always chatting away happily,
He is the afternoon when the sun is setting,
He is a grape bursting with energy,
He is purple, one minute calm, the next, very energetic,
Like a tornado sucking up houses and trees,
A chimp chattering away happily.

Jonathan Dennis (8)
St James' CE Junior School, Tunbridge Wells

WHEN SPRING ARRIVED

When spring arrived,
it made me so happy.
Spring is the season of life,
everyone loves the mornings of spring,
how it makes the birds sing.
Oh, spring makes me so happy.

Jacinta Race-Lyons (8)
St James' CE Junior School, Tunbridge Wells

COLOURS

What is purple?
Purple is my dad shouting at me with great fury
and the fireworks going *boom!*

What is green?
Green is the birds cheeping and singing
in the sunlit forest
and the fish jumping happily out of the sea.

What is black?
Black is the ugly monster staring at you
making you very scared
and it's your tummy when you go on a roller coaster.

Edmund Osborn (9)
St James' CE Junior School, Tunbridge Wells

I NEED MORE!

I want this,
I want that,
I want cookies
And a big, fluffy cat.

I want those,
I want them,
I want chocolate
And a shiny red gem.

I want him,
I want her,
I want strawberries
And coat made of fur.

I want Barbie,
I want Ken,
I want some piglets
In a piglet pen.

I need this,
I need that,
I need everything
And that is that!

So where is it then?

Emily Simkins (11)
St James' CE Junior School, Tunbridge Wells

ALICE

Alice is a TV
Sometimes talking, sometimes not,
She's the middle of the day
Playful and always moving,
A sweet apple
Bright and strong,
She's purple like a kite
Floating in the air,
A dolphin
Swimming in the sea
And the sun
Joyful and hot.

Nicola Mian (8)
St James' CE Junior School, Tunbridge Wells

RABBITS

R   abbits are so soft and furry
A   rabbit hops high up in the blue sky
B   right colours of their fur, brown and grey
B   eautiful rabbits hide in their dirty homes
I   saw a rabbit sitting on a very wet bench
T   he rabbits saw the yellow sun go down
S   o I have to say goodbye to the rabbits and you,
                    Bye bye.

Katie Clark (8)
St James' CE Junior School, Tunbridge Wells

DAISY

Daisy is a calm, ticking clock
moving slowly,
The middle of the day
when the sun is burning,
A big, juicy orange,
A light blue sky
when the sun is dying,
A warm summer's day
in the morning,
A guinea pig making lots of noise.

Harriet Waghorn (9)
St James' CE Junior School, Tunbridge Wells

ALICE

My little sister is a lamp,
Usually happy but sometimes sad,
She's like 9 o'clock in the morning,
Lively and wide awake,
A plum, she's always so sweet,
Like a scaly green rattlesnake,
Always noisy and eating things,
Like blue, she's always got lots of energy,
She's like a very hot sunny day.

Oscar Whitaker (8)
St James' CE Junior School, Tunbridge Wells

COLOUR

What is red?
Red is a bull charging at a small scarlet sheet
And an old crumbling skyscraper, exploding with dynamite.

What is black?
Black is a wet pavement
And a bird's feather.

What is yellow?
Yellow is mouldy orange peel
And the burning sun in the middle of the day.

Ashley Nailor (9)
St James' CE Junior School, Tunbridge Wells

MY SISTER IS . . .

My sister is brightly coloured curtains
fluttering in the breeze.
My sister is the early morning
when the birds are singing.
My sister is a rosy red apple
juicy and sweet.
My sister is a hot summer's day in the park
with children playing.
My sister is a fluffy guinea pig
playful and sweet.

Jasmine Ravandi (8)
St James' CE Junior School, Tunbridge Wells

MR CHANDLER

Mr Chandler is like a radiator,
his warmth always turned on
to heat you up.

He is an afternoon person,
getting calmer as the day passes.

A pumpkin planting seeds
into every bad person.

Lilac, kind and caring
all day through.

A soft blowing wind which will
drive away all your troubles.

If you are a sad kitten,
he is waiting to find you
and make you happy again.

Severine Goddard (8)
St James' CE Junior School, Tunbridge Wells

WOODS

Trees are green
Woodcutters are mean

Mud is lumpy
The path is bumpy

Leaves on the ground
A lot of animals to be found.

Philip Peacock (11)
St James' CE Junior School, Tunbridge Wells

FURNITURE POEM
(A poem about Georgina McMaster)

The person is like a golden TV
The time of the day is when she is watching TV
She is like a hairy coconut
The weather would be bright lightning
The person is like a cheetah.

Joshua Willis (8)
St James' CE Junior School, Tunbridge Wells

JOE

Joe is a sofa with a soft heart,
He is midday, the time that everybody is so lively,
A banana with lots of energy,
Yellow, always cheerful and bright,
A happy day, chattering and bouncing,
He is a fox sneaking about and tricking us.

George Offer (9)
St James' CE Junior School, Tunbridge Wells

MY BIG BROTHER

My big brother is like a sofa being moved around all the time.
He is like the night because he is not very lively.
Like an apple rolling about in the sizzling sun.
He is like red because he thinks he is boss.
A thunderstorm when lightning is coming down from the sky.
Like a lion fighting for a win.

Nicky Reilly (8)
St James' CE Junior School, Tunbridge Wells

FLOWERS

F   lowers are everywhere in your garden
L   ips from tulips and dils from daffodils
O   ver hills we grow in neat, straight rows
W ith sparkling petals and bright green stalks
E   merald coloured leaves and ruby coloured petals
R   ampaging forests, we slowly brighten up the dark green wood
S   adly now we say goodbye but we'll be back, bye bye.

Liane Abrams (8)
St James' CE Junior School, Tunbridge Wells

THE NINE PLANETS

Far away in another world
There are two planets named Earth and Mars
Nearby they're surrounded by stars
Mercury can see the biggest of them
Whilst in Jupiter they're jolly men.

Pluto is the furthest away
And Saturn lies in its bright colours all day.

Young aliens from Neptune, Uranus and Venus
Shout back - aren't you glad you've seen us?

These are the nine planets
Maybe there are some we haven't discovered yet
We shall find out in years to come
When they're found we will be done.

Celia Smith (10)
St John's CE Junior School, Tunbridge Wells

THE ALIEN

It was tall and green
with jaws looking at me.
Its claws were the size of bananas,
they were red with blood.
It had red eyes
it was . . .
it was an alien.

Joe Byrne
St John's CE Junior School, Tunbridge Wells

A FLYING RAINBOW

What is it, where's it come from?
It's a flying rainbow.
Look at the colours sparkling in the sky.
There was a whooshing sound
It jerked upwards and flew into darkness.
It was a shooting star.

Harriet Jowitt (9)
St John's CE Junior School, Tunbridge Wells

THE MOON

The air all still and silent
The planet all deserted with no life
The moon is like a piece of silver paper
Shining in the darkness.

Karl Muhs (9)
St John's CE Junior School, Tunbridge Wells

THE MOON

I asked my dad if he remembered
the first man landing on the moon.
When I went to bed that night
I sat in my bed looking at the moon
I sat looking into the night.
That morning at school my teacher asked me
If I knew what date it was that man landed on the moon.
I knew straight away that it was 21st July 1969
And his name was Neil Armstrong from America.
That night I sat in my bed and again,
Looked up to the full moon
And wondered what it would be like
To be the first man to step on the moon.

Stephanie Turner (9)
St John's CE Junior School, Tunbridge Wells

TOUCH

I like the cold feel of my new bike
I like the feel of my fluffy Winnie The Pooh
I like the smoothness of concrete steps
I like the leathery feel of my pencil case
I like the fluffy feel of my bunny rabbit
I like the soft feel of my bed
I like the roughness of my new carpet
I like the crispy feel of a leaf
I like the smooth feel of chocolate
I like the smoothness of the wooden door
I like the smoothness of metal
The feel of a clock.

Freddie Farnie (7)
St John's CE Junior School, Tunbridge Wells

WHO ARE THEY?

A body so green like a tree!
A waddle so unstable like a penguin!
A smooth belly, so smooth like a ripe apple - fresh and green.
Their eyes staring at me like I am the answer to their dream.

I don't know if I'll see them again
All I know is that this memory will be treasured
With me forever!

Daisy Lockheart (10)
St John's CE Junior School, Tunbridge Wells

SMELL

I like the smell of newly cut grass
and the fresh leaves of autumn.
I like the perfume of red and white roses
and turned over earth.
I like the smell of burning wood
at my grandad's house
when we have bonfires
and the sweet smell of apples and pears.

Joe McKinlay (8)
St John's CE Junior School, Tunbridge Wells

A ROCKET

A rocket with the warmth of a blazing fire
With the warm colours of red, orange and yellow
Coming out of the exhaust

The quickness makes it look like a shooting star
Flying across the black winter sky.

A rocket is a pencil doing a dot-to-dot
Through the amazing Milky Way.

A rocket is a pointed dart
Sailing through the air to hit the bullseye.

Alexander Hookway (9)
St John's CE Junior School, Tunbridge Wells

TOUCH

I like to feel the smoothness of a pebble on the beach
A lovely warm bath
The sticky feeling of sweat
The furriness of McTavish, my bear
And the fluffiness of felt
The prickliness of a pineapple
And the flatness of paper.

Rohan Thorniley (7)
St John's CE Junior School, Tunbridge Wells

TOUCH

I like to feel the roughness of the autumn leaves
when I kick them on my walk.
I like to feel the smoothness of my rabbit's fur
when I stroke him.
I like to feel the warmth of my fire
when I sit close to it.
I like to feel the cool, fresh air
when I play in the garden.
I hate the feel of rain soaking in my socks.

Sarah Matchett (7)
St John's CE Junior School, Tunbridge Wells

TOUCH

I like to feel the roughness of a pine tree
when I lean against it.

I like to feel the smoothness of ice cream
when it slides down my throat.

I like to feel the warmth of my bed
when I wake up on a freezing morning.

I like to feel the cool of a fan
blowing across my face.

I hate to feel conkers falling on my head.

Joe Cray (7)
St John's CE Junior School, Tunbridge Wells

CAN YOU IMAGINE

Can you imagine in your head,
Being a person during the war, snuggled up in bed?
Bleak and perishing, skin blood-red raw,
Too apprehensive to approach the towering door.

The horrifying noise of air raids clanging in my ear
I stumble outside, the blasting gale is giving a piercing seer.
My life is ruined and in the shelter, immobile I lay
Struggling, clambering, *'Warmth'* I gasp, unable to say
'Mummy, no, don't go to the ghastly screeching sound.'
Tranquil outside, cautiously I poke out my head
Mum is on the ground, a massive crater lying beside her
Everything is a confusing blur.

That's the way I think of it, in the time of war,
Can you describe it or are you not sure?

Daisy McInnerney (10)
Sundridge & Brasted CE Primary School

HOLIDAYS

Splishing, splashing of the blue sea
I hope it's still waiting for me
I wonder if it will rain here
Dad, let us go and find the pier.

We got a house near the seaside
Watch out for all the great big tides
I am going to sunbathe here
I hope the newsagent's is near.

We are all watching animals
There are lots and lots of mammals
Look at that fluffy, huge lion
Watch out for that piece of iron.

It is time to go home today
I wish very much that we could stay
It will be late when we get home
I brush my hair with a comb.

Lisa Vagg (10)
Sundridge & Brasted CE Primary School

THE HUGE TOWN OF LONDON

Busy people in a busy town
Cars waiting while lights are changing colour
While men and women are crossing at the lights
Getting in your way, so many people.

Homeless people living on the street
Rubbish everywhere, all on the floor
High and low buildings all around the town
Men and women rushing to get to work.

Lisa Bristow (10)
Sundridge & Brasted CE Primary School

BLITZ

B ombs come whooshing down as they light up the night sky
L ondon is being bombed, homes being torn down
I was shocked at the sight of my village flaring up with flames
T he stars glittered in the sky as the planes flew down
Z oom, a bomb landed heavy on my home as I watched my home
being burnt down.

Naomi Murray (8)
Sundridge & Brasted CE Primary School

THE BLITZ

B ombs flying across the night sky
L ights on, close the curtains!
I nside the dark and gloomy shelter
T here's a knock on the old rotten door
Z ip, zap my house is gone!

Dean Vagg (9)
Sundridge & Brasted CE Primary School

BLITZ

B ombs were falling from the sky
L anding on the houses
I t was scary
T here were some lights on
Z oom, bang, crash.

Hannah Logan (8)
Sundridge & Brasted CE Primary School

THE BLITZ

The Second World War began
Everyone had a gas mask and bombs were dropped
Everyone rushed in to get their gas masks
Surprisingly no gas was dropped
Each day you hoped the war was over
Can you hear the air raid siren?
Oh no, not again
Nice one Hitler
Dad has joined the army
Will it end
Or will it go on forever?
Rotten Hitler
Let's get him
Dad will be home now . . .

Liam Bristow (8)
Sundridge & Brasted CE Primary School

THE GREYHOUND

The dog ran as fast as he could
And he stopped and hopped
From the distance
People saying run.

The hare going round twice
The cheering loudly of the crowd above
Dogs running round and round
Dogs barking
Coming closer and closer.

Daniel Corp (9)
Sundridge & Brasted CE Primary School

THE STREAM

Down by the sparkling stream
So relaxing, it's like a dream.
Birds are singing high in the trees
On nearby flowers are busy bees.
Freezing cold water so crystal clear
It's calm here with nothing to fear.

Trickling water, shiny and fast
Only the sound of a fisherman's cast.
The morning's cold but bright
The sun's reflecting like a light.
Shiny but almost still
I watch the river fill.

What is that I begin to hear?
Only mother duck with babies near.
Swimming slowly, swimming fast
Making me smile as they go past.
Dragonflies darting about the stream
What lovely colours, blue and green.

Megan Tunnicliffe (10)
Sundridge & Brasted CE Primary School

THE BLITZ

A   cross the world they flew
I   t was the way to do it
R   umbling into London.

R   ed alert! Red alert!
A   bomb is sizzling
I   t is ready to be dropped
D   ad look, the church is bombed!

James Wootton (7)
Sundridge & Brasted CE Primary School

BLITZ

B ang, whizz, I heard a loud crash
O h I hear noisy loud bangs
M y heart was pounding like a person wetting himself
B ut I rushed out of my house. That was it,
            my house exploded.

Maxine Marlin (8)
Sundridge & Brasted CE Primary School

THE BLITZ

B ombs are coming you don't know where
O r you don't know when
M en are dead and men are fighting
B ombs are coming you don't know where
S irens are going off.

Ashley Scott (8)
Sundridge & Brasted CE Primary School

THE BLITZ

B ang, disaster has struck London
L ondon is full of flames
I 'm really desperately hungry
T here's a knock at the door
Z ip zap our house was gone!

Anna Geer (8)
Sundridge & Brasted CE Primary School

FEEDING A DOLPHIN

I grabbed a handful of food
The dolphin was in a mood
The grub was yellow and rough
The grey-black dolphin was tough.

The dolphin went bonkers
And some water went on the sand,
I got so very damp
The dolphin looked like a tramp.

The dolphin slowly calmed down
Soon the food got old and brown
And I had to throw it away
I hurled it over the bay.

I snatched some more dolphin feed
It was made of tiny seeds
I gave the dolphin the food
And no more was he that crude.

Sarah Comb (9)
Sundridge & Brasted CE Primary School

MALDIVES

Extremely calm, never *booms*
What a cool, funny adventure.
Water was calm and crystal clear
Bright white moon, never grey.

Fishes were pretty, luminous
Coral reefs were beautiful too.
Tropical beaches, fine, white, sand.
We had a generous waiter.

There was a miniature pool
I thought I was dreaming it.
It was lovely, I loved it.
The food was weird, I hated it.

As soon as we got there I smiled.
I thought it was fabulous, great.
I went out snorkelling, pretty.
Could it be real? Yes it can be.

Rebecca Swift (9)
Sundridge & Brasted CE Primary School

DEVON

The cove was enormous
Fine and sparkly sand
Chilly and green sea
Towering high sand dunes

Hot, creamy custard
Flaming hot apple pie
Greasy, battered cod
Salty, warm chips

The snazzy coloured yacht
Just out of the harbour
Floating on the shimmering sea
It stood out from all the rest

The small, chubby foals
Grazing in the meadow
The orangy tabby cat
Washing itself in the sun.

Daniel Shuttleworth (10)
Sundridge & Brasted CE Primary School

LOGRONO

Logrono is not a crowded site,
With hardly any wildlife
And only a field of grape bushes,
The views are quite magnificent,
But would be better without the haze.

It is midday and very hot,
We need a lot of cold refreshments,
I think it's extremely clammy,
Mostly built up on deserty land,
It's very dry, dusty and hot.

On the way back after a fine day,
The thunder clouds are overhead,
Flashes of lightning and thunder booms,
Dramatic sights I'll never forget,
It was extremely enjoyable.

Michael Keogh (10)
Sundridge & Brasted CE Primary School

BLITZ

S   wastika flags are waving
P   ictures of Union Jacks are waving
I   think England will win the war
T   ommy guns are shooting
F   ires start spreading
I   think Germany started the war
R   uined houses all over the place
E   veryone is frightened!

Thomas McInnerney (8)
Sundridge & Brasted CE Primary School

THE SURPRISE

At the pet department store, there it lay
one little guinea pig I liked that day,
but left it for a moment lying there,
while I looked around at the other fare.

Round the corner something caught my eye,
two little guinea pigs small and shy.
Hiding in their hay and just staying warm
waiting for someone to notice their charm.

We bought some food and the bedding hay,
they are going to be my pets today.
We got them home and safely in their hutch,
they were small and furry and soft to touch.

Jonathan Pardoe (9)
Sundridge & Brasted CE Primary School

ANIMAL ANTICS

Slimy, spooky, slithering snakes,
Sneaking into some caves,
Sneaky, crafty sea lions,
Splashing over waves.
Jumping, leaping, springing monkeys,
Swinging from leaves to trees!

Shiny, stinging, flying birds,
Zooming through the air,
Fiery, stripy, blackish tigers,
Rushing like a bear!

Anthony Mason (8)
Warren Road Primary School

WINTER

Church bells ring,
Robins sing,
Christmas has arrived,
The snow is here,
White as ever,
Children love going out
Ready to race on their toboggans.

The Christmas trees are shining
With presents underneath,
The decorations hang from their leaves
Shimmering in delight,
Hot chocolate is sipped
By cosy adults sitting by the glowing fire.

Rachel Glass (8)
Warren Road Primary School

MY RABBIT POEM

My rabbit is happy and bouncy,
Her ears are floppy and fluffy,
She is very wild and sneaky
When she wants to,
She's warm with her fur.
Rabbits have big, furry feet,
My rabbit is very funny
And she is ticklish.
She is sweet when she eats carrots.
Why do rabbits have bobbly tails?

Bryony May Palmer (8)
Warren Road Primary School

SANTA CLAUS

One cold, frosty night,
Santa Claus came in sight,
Some children crept and peeked and saw,
His snowy white beard through the door.
The strange man said,
'Ho! Ho! Ho!'
And a merry Christmas to you Joe.
As he slipped through the door,
The children followed him
Crawling on the floor.
He ate the cookies, we didn't care,
The children were too tired to stand or stare.

Poppy Ballantyne (8)
Warren Road Primary School

ENTERING A CITY

The cars are fierce, tormenting lions trapping the road,
Noisy traffic like howling beasts and fierce tigers,
People in cars fed up, like bored tigers,
The leaves are off the trees with crinkly, crunchy leaves,
Leaves falling off the trees when people rush past.
The beast of London is here,
Offices working, busy bees at work,
Everybody's rushing around like a herd of sheep.
The day has ended, everyone goes home,
Now the town is as quiet and as calm as a mouse.

Kirsty Wade (9)
Warren Road Primary School

ENTERING A CITY

Angry faces
In insect-like cars
Show they want out.
Unwanted shops
Start to crumble away
Graffiti plasters the walls
High buildings shout out
Their importance.
Lifeless cars wait
Not talking
Young families rush
But old citizens wobble humbly.
Old cinemas are hardly used
And small blocks of flats
Get larger as we travel on.

Rebecca Costin (10)
Warren Road Primary School

ENTERING A CITY

Cars shoot like rockets
Down the frosty, musty road
Like a flash of lightning
The trees are bare
With no leaves
Like stripped naked bodies
In the freezing cold
People scatter like leaves
Through the busy street of London
The trees have got no leaves
I wish all the colours
Would come back to me.

Hannah Wood (9)
Warren Road Primary School

MR WARREN-AXE'S DESK

'15p a peep, feel inside
For you will feel a dirty tissue
15p a peep' he announced.

I stumbled towards his desk
Feeling very anxious
Carefully does it
'15p a peep' he called.

I peered into the desk
I saw with disbelief
A great big hairy hand
'15p a peep' he quickly cried.

I heard from within the desk
Nails scraping on the blackboard
And crunching of crisps
'15p a peep.'

I sniffed around
And what was that I could smell?
Rotten eggs and frogs' legs
I had the impression that
It was going to jump out at me.

Francesca Preocanin (10)
Warren Road Primary School

JOY

Joy is light blue and tastes like ice cream
Joy looks like a boy playing with action figures
It smells like roasted burgers
It makes me feel really happy.

Scott Wakeford (8)
Warren Road Primary School

ENTERING A CITY

Angry faces like stone-cold steel
On expensive mobile phones
As the old folk
Hobble past
Laughing children
On their way to school
Street cleaners whistle
As they sweep
Along the pavement way
The slow, huddled traffic
No faster than ants
Pollutes the air
With fumes
The beautiful shops leap out
Against the ugly, tumbled way
A crying baby
Sucking a dummy in a pram
Hoping for a lolly
Translucent windows
On tower blocks tall
Shine blue in the midday sun.

Robert A Filer (10)
Warren Road Primary School

AUTUMN

The cold breeze in the air
Leaves swaying down from trees
Animals hibernating
Squirrels running in the breeze.

Snails in their hard shell
Hedgehogs all bristly,
The sun is peeking through the clouds
Rain is all tingly.

Squirrels, brown and grey
Foxes running over dark roads
Cars with their flash lights on
No sight of frogs or toads.

Charlotte Jacobs (9)
Warren Road Primary School

MR WARREN-AXE'S DESK

The din inside his desk,
Is making me very curious,
Although he charges £12 a peep,
I would still pay once or twice!

Whatever's in there
Eats disgusting things,
Like rotten eggs and mouldy apples,
Which give off a foul smell!

Once I stuck my hand down the hole
And I pulled out a soggy tissue,
Which he always keeps in his desk,
Which reminds him of the first tooth
That came out.

I saw him pull out a mouldy sandwich once,
He looked around,
He put his jaws around it
And bit!

Once I paid his expensive fee,
I opened his tray,
I glanced behind his books
And I saw . . .

Ralph Yea (10)
Warren Road Primary School

THE DAYS OF THE WEEK

On Monday mornings I hear a din;
the dustmen are a-coming to empty all the bins.
On Tuesday mornings as I go downstairs
my sister follows with enormous care.
On Wednesday mornings it is pouring down
so winter will come again.
On Thursday mornings it's cold and misty
the trees are swaying and it's frosty.
On Friday mornings we go to school
but then I go swimming in the pool.
On Saturday mornings I sleep in late
but then I have to take Mum to the station.
On Sunday mornings I lay in snoring
but Daddy's awake and he's up early.

Lacey Nutt (9)
Warren Road Primary School

A COACH RIDE

Trees are bare and brown
Children playing, screaming loud like the noisiest hyenas
In this bumpy monster on wheels
Swerving on roads, moving around
Hurting our heads on the window
Cars as fast as a cheetah
Streets busy with mums and prams
Restaurants making us thirsty and hungry as we go along
The smelly petrol stations with groaning cars
The noisy bells with the howling wind
The end of the journey is very near
The British museum, our hopes rise!
We are glad to get off this sticky machine.

Jessica Woollaston (9)
Warren Road Primary School

PATRICK'S DESK

One pound a peep, Patrick pleaded,
I paid my money, I know it's a rip-off
But I wanted to see what it was in his desk.

Smelling of mouldy apples, garlic and even worse,
Rotten eggs.
Lucy reported that Patrick's desk smelt of a farm.

Lucy and I heard noises like nails scraping
Up and down a chalk board
And a bag of crisps being crunched by something.

We both saw black claws and nibbled away pencil sharpenings,
old bread and a pile of brown hair.

I opened the desk top and slid my hand inside,
I felt some sticky stuff and stroked a . . .

Tareg Morris (10)
Warren Road Primary School

FAST CAR

We all glanced at the car calmly as the monster of the road
                    roared past all the busy streets.
We didn't see it at first but then we saw it.
It was as fast as a lightning flash.
We had never seen anything as horrific as it.
It roared past all the dusty and disgusting alleys.
All of the people were the same.
He whizzed past all of the petrol stations
And all of the restaurants and all of the theatres.
The monsters speeding over the grey sea with lines on them.
It will never be the same.

Alistair O'Dwyer (9)
Warren Road Primary School

A BUSY CITY

Zooming past trees and skyscrapers
makes all the leaves fall down.
Gigantic buildings up above me
looks like the giant of the streets.
Trees swaying like the wind.
Colourful leaves from the rainbow over me.
Trees bare in the autumn,
leaves changing when they fall to the ground.

More yellow taxis with people in them
rushing about like a swarm of bees.

Brum, brum shakes the houses high
brum, brum a shake again
made the waiter jump and drop his tray again.

As the coach went slowly past
I saw the place we were going to.
Hooray, hooray, this is the place!
The city is very busy today.

Sarah Bradbury (9)
Warren Road Primary School

FEAR

It feels dark like blood
It tastes like lava
It smells like rotten apples
It looks like a devil's cave
With lava
It sounds spooky with a piano
It feels like you're in a devil's cave.

Danny Thrussell
Warren Road Primary School

WINTER

Brown crispy leaves, smelly old garbage on the ground,
stinky pollution in the air.
The air as cold as ice, people chattering their teeth,
you wouldn't believe how cold it is.

It's the middle of winter, the shops have got Christmas presents.
Busy shoppers getting huge presents.
In town centres Christmas decorations are up,
they've got beautiful colours though.

It's Christmas, children getting up early - very excited indeed.
Stockings all stiff and hard because of all the very hard presents.
Adults very tired, want to go to bed.

As a new year comes and goes
people have fireworks and stay up till midnight.
As Big Ben strikes 12, a new day has come.
People say 'Good morning'.

Ben Norley (9)
Warren Road Primary School

MADNESS

Monsters roar down the road.
A rush of wind from the train as it rides past the station.
Leaves blowing in the old street as the people walk past.
All the shops are dead as the wind blows.
Trees swaying like a boy on a swing.
Big cars and little monsters zoom down the road.
Police are off in a flash as they zoom after the bad guys.
Graffiti on the walls of London.

Michael Lloyd (9)
Warren Road Primary School

INTO THE CITY

The black cat is like a roaring lion
The people in the cars are very tired and bored
                                because of the traffic.
There is a lot of noisy traffic.
People hooting their hooters,
Very busy streets.
Garbage on the ground
Dirty alleys and dirty streets.
London is a very busy place, especially when there are
                                a lot of people.
Graffiti is like snails leaving their slimy tracks behind.
The streets are as busy as bees.
People are rushing around like swarms of wasps
Some people are walking around very slowly, like snails.
Cars storming past the town like rockets.
People roaming the streets like monsters
Aeroplanes flying like birds.
Lots of sweet wrappers on the ground,
Traffic lights - green, yellow, red
Lots of dirty streets with garbage on the ground.

James Foxen (9)
Warren Road Primary School

DIRTY LONDON

The brown trees with crinkly leaves on the floor
                                like crunched up paper.
I saw a black cat and it was fat.
Its dusty and dirty floor - people sweeping up to your doors.
The streets are as dusty as horrible dustbins.
We are zooming home.
We are very tired.

Larissa Paritt (9)
Warren Road Primary School

GOING INTO THE CITY

Graffiti has been sprayed on the walls
like slimy snails leaving their tracks behind them.
The streets are crowded,
everyone seems to be going somewhere
                                        like a swam of bees.
People are trying to catch the monster
of the tracks as it strolls by.
Aeroplanes fly high in the sky, like birds.
In Trafalgar Square there are pigeons,
leaves are on the floor being kicked around children.
It's blue up above, like the sea,
trees swaying in the cold icy wind.
Dogs being walked by their owners on a lead.
Tower Bridge is high.
Then the London Eye came into sight.

Chloe Robertson (9)
Warren Road Primary School

BUSY LONDON

Lots of officers working busily away as busy as bees.
Piles of paper
Scattered like the monster of the wind just blew in.
Oh! Enormous London!

The minotour of the sky blowing, swish!
Swaying the clusters of trees.
Stardust falling from fairies
spreading magic all around.
Oh! Enormous London!

Susanna Nallamilli (9)
Warren Road Primary School

SEEING LONDON

The building my dad worked in
has lots of windows
and is very tall,
like a snake going up to the sky.
Old Kent Road is very, very busy
and is a long ancient road.
The traffic is noisy
and the garbage is smelly,
like a dirty animal.
The Elephant and Castle is giant and great.
The Imperial War Museum
with its canon is like a long giraffe
lying on the ground.

Robert Stanton (9)
Warren Road Primary School

GOING INTO THE CITY

As I went into London I saw . . .

A great many people rushing through
the streets, swift as arrows.

Trains stopping in stations like dragons,
stopping in their lairs.
And drains like vacuum cleaners,
sweeping up the muck and dust.

The lamps at night, stare at the people walking past
whilst they in turn, stare at the graffiti,
the slimy snail trails.

Joe Daniel Thomas (9)
Warren Road Primary School

LOVE

Love is light pink
and tastes wonderfully sweet
like a pink lolly.
Smelling of a garden of flowers.
Love looks like two butterflies
together in the sky.
Love sounds like birds singing
and feels like kissing.

Emma Jayne Crawford (8)
Warren Road Primary School

LOVE

Love is light red like a red rose
And it tastes like a cup full of red wine.
It smells of a nice vase full of roses
And it looks like a wonderful dressed child.
It sounds like a beautiful harp
And it makes me happy.

Charlotte Woollard (9)
Warren Road Primary School

LOVE

Love is bright pink.
It tastes like sweet peas.
It looks like people going out with each other.
It sounds like robins dancing in the moonlight.
It feels like fun.

Akika Kalde (9)
Warren Road Primary School

ENTERING A CITY

Entering a city
I see
People in cars like statues
Sitting, waiting to be knocked down,
Children hurrying to school
Like mice avoiding cats,
People with bags of important work,
Builders struggling to lift bricks
Like timid rats,
People in queues wait angrily,
Anxious to show their faces at meetings.

Traffic stops, people gulp,
Postman late delivering post,
Cars in queues make people mad,
Motorbikes like snakes slither through cars.

A block of flats
Yellow like bees' honey,
Another with hanging rays,
Houses burnt like an orphanage,
Dilapidated buildings being rebuilt,
Offices towering over car parks,
A grand, icy building
With a clear waterfall,
Sprinkles tears of water.
Buildings around,
The theme's like a kingdom of money.

Isabelle Mongelard (10)
Warren Road Primary School

ENTERING A CITY

People crowd the railway station
Hurrying to catch a train,
Some people stand as still as stone,
Others run like frantic ants.

A glass building like a block of ice
Sprinkles fountains of water,
Like grains of rice.
Blocks of flats are very tall,
Although inside are depressingly small.

The buildings at the edge of the Thames
Without a barrier to hold them up,
Look like they're about to fall.

Stranded drivers sigh heavily,
As pedestrians just walk on by.

Sophie Bailey (10)
Warren Road Primary School

LOVE

Love is bright pink
And tastes like sweets
So gentle and chewy
Smelling like strong perfume.
Love looks beautifully fragile
And sounds so romantic.
Love feels sweet and soft
Like a cosy pillow.

Adam Hughes (9)
Warren Road Primary School

THE BUSY CITY

As we move through the giant city
Sweeping through the dusty roads we see;
Towering tower blocks watching the city
Busy cars roaring like tigers of the jungle,
Never stopping, never stopping.

Huge restaurants belting out smoke,
Gloomy shops stripped from their signs
Busy bees rushing around
Never stopping, never stopping.

Trees stripped from all their leaves
Deserted shops, no owners
Busy shops carpeted with people,
Never stopping, never stopping.

Caroline Blanchard (9)
Warren Road Primary School

ENTERING A CITY

People pleading like kids or lambs
Departed from their mothers
Most people wealthy, not caring about the poor
Distressed people tensely sit in roaring cars
Like electric drills.
Traffic is rumbling like an erupting volcano
Lorries are booming, buses bouncing up and down
When they stop.
Funeral cars like birds, glide along.
Boarded up shops with vile graffiti everywhere.
Looming over every building is St Paul's Cathedral.
Over cars and shops, blooms a skyscraper.

Patrick Wells (10)
Warren Road Primary School

ENTERING A CITY

I see grey, ghostly faces behind windscreens,
Weirdly transparent and white.
I see straight, serious faces.

Bodies marching, hands clutching briefcases,
Fat with a hundred papers
And children being tugged along on toddler reins,
Like shaggy Shetland ponies.

Multicoloured ants scuttle along the road
While other people sweat and strain,
Trying to work out spreadsheets.

Old, grey buildings, covered in graffiti,
Plastered over the badly painted walls,
Like some grotesque art form.

Zoe Shute (10)
Warren Road Primary School

ENTERING A CITY

The birds are like the flying gods of high up.
The cars are the road monsters speeding down the road.
The buildings are as high as high could be.
The people in the street rushing around like busy bees.
The sticky stuff gets stuck to your shoe and won't come off.
Cats running when the barker comes along the road.
The fire in the sky is always flaming hot.
The crispy leaves crunching and snapping when you tread on them.
The trains zooming past like a rocket in the sky.

Robert Brown (9)
Warren Road Primary School

ENTERING A CITY

Lady jogger passing by
All in orange, stands out in the crowd
Angry businessmen in their cars
Stuck in traffic looking miserable
Light turns green, faces look happier
People running for buses, late for work
Suitcases clashing
Looking colder as the chill bites them
Taxis waiting in the queue
Like a school of fish
People jumping in, off to work
Colourful cars like pots of paint
Three wheeled cars bopping up and down like jelly
New cars, old cars taking their owners
To supermarkets, work or even school
Shops ready for Christmas, decorated with lights
County pubs all around
Indian Tandoori, hair stylists
Glass building like an ice palace
Twinkling in the sunlight
Parades of shops, some neglected, some looked after
A house covered in paintings of flowers
Red, green, yellow, blue
Orange cranes very bright
Sainsbury's petrol station
Looks like a pirate ship
Crispy leaves
Red, gold, bronze, brown
Flocks of birds fly to and fro
Flapping their wings like fans
Wheels stacked up on the pavement
With patterns like stars
Colossal Catford cat placed on signpost
Looks realistic

Dilapidated buildings being built again
Wouldn't like to live there
Just going into Old Kent Road
The longest road in London
Passing the Red Elephant and Castle
Then a gigantic cinema in Waterloo
Held up by strings
Screen all around
London Eye slowly turning
Like a fairground wheel
Over the Thames we go
Under the BBC Centre
Bumpy ride
Open top buses, people looking cold
We're here!

Sarah McGuire (10)
Warren Road Primary School

A BUSY CITY

Frantic people running around
Like ants in an ant hill.
Cars rush by like a flash of lightning
And alleyways as dark and bare as a tunnel.

Busy shoppers rushing around
Like swarms of bees.
Annoyed people arguing with traffic wardens
Because they get parking fees.

Joshua Foley (9)
Warren Road Primary School

ENTERING A CITY

Scurrying people
Clutch together like glue,
Cold children
Stick to their mothers
Before they catch a cold.

Stone vehicles
Have no sign of moving
Angry faces
Scrunched up like a trunk of a tree.

Places people plead to go
With constant beeping
From grumpy cars,
At an everlasting red, regular amber
But rare green.

Eloise Kendall (10)
Warren Road Primary School

JOY

Joy is twilight blue
It tastes nice
Like blueberries
It smells fresh
Like bluebells
It looks pretty
It sounds joyful
Joy makes me feel happy.

Sarah Worwood (9)
Warren Road Primary School

ENTERING A CITY

Roads are running
Never stopping,
Long, large sticks
Stand lost,
Coloured shapes
Stand still
Honking sharply.
Small insect-like creatures scurry
Ignoring everything
Not a sound made.
Buildings stand grand,
Shops covered with graffiti
While old buildings crumble away,
Flats keep on growing
Some look grand,
Other frail.
One building stands out above all
Shining with its glamour
As the sun glows high above
The palace looks like ice.

Rebecca Benfield (10)
Warren Road Primary School

ENTERING A CITY

People swarm in and out of each other
Scattering like antelope fleeing a cheetah's grasp.
Deserted buildings stand lonely and neglected
Scarred by graffiti
Others stand proud with hundreds of windows
And the power to change the world.

Tony Onodi (10)
Warren Road Primary School

CHARLOTTE'S DESK!

'10p a peek!' shouted Charlotte
Chloe put her hand inside
And she felt an old, sticky toffee
Then a soggy old tissue,
But then at last she felt
Claws of a hairy hand!

Then Alexander came
And looked inside a hole,
Quickly he jumped back
Because a hairy hand came out,
With an old piece of bread
Which looked mouldy indeed.

Sarah put her ear to Charlotte's desk
And heard the crunching of crisps,
But then nails scraping down a chalk board
What could it be?
Sarah heard something else
But it wasn't from the desk,
It was only the dinner bell
For year three to go in to lunch.

Next was Phillip
He lifted up the lid of the desk
And smelt a funny smell of rotten eggs,
Mouldy apples and sweets.
But the worst of all was garlic,
Phewww!
Boy, was that a disgusting smell
It sure was
And Sarah nearly fainted.

Finally all of them felt quite sick
They lifted up the desk lid,
Looked behind the books
Even in an ink pot
And there it was . . .
The naughty, horrible . . .

Charlotte Farquhar (9)
Warren Road Primary School

OUT IN LONDON

In the busy street of London
people are working like bees
buzzing angrily in disagreement.
Rubbish piling up like germs
spreading everywhere, spewing its poison
like a slimy sewer.
Cars flying by, like a flash of lightning
roaming across our roads.
The monsters of the road spoiling it.
Flashy cars, old cars whizzing by
like a cheetah in a race.
Beautiful buildings, gigantic buildings
standing paralysed like the king of trees.
People walking swift and steady
scattering down the road.
Birds swooping as fast as any
seeking for something to eat
like the king of birds flying
swiftly and proudly.
Leaves falling down from the trees
scattering gently down the street of London.

Thomas Hodson (9)
Warren Road Primary School

ENTERING A CITY

Flats with green roofs and blue balconies,
New buildings being built,
Bright shops and dull shops,
Rows of A4 paper.
All the different buildings around
The Thames,
Buses and cars sitting in traffic
While the traffic lights change
Red, green, amber.
All the different makes of vehicles
Pass quickly and slowly.
Lots of pleased faces
Inside the hand car wash shops
And a young man sitting on a bench
Having a cigarette, looking depressed.
A smart woman catching a bus,
Small children playing on
Expensive bikes.

Rebecca Feddon (10)
Warren Road Primary School

ENTERING A CITY

Lifeless people
Strolling the streets,
Saying nothing
Others stand at the bus stops
Like ghosts.

Row after row of coloured cars
Like a cloudy rainbow
On the ground
Grumpy people
Wishing they weren't late for work.

Dirty flats
With graffiti all over
A few houses with bars on
Like a cage
But to keep people out.

Charlotte Burgoyne (10)
Warren Road Primary School

ENTERING A CITY

One hundred mile an hour cars
Just sitting there
Still as blades of grass
Unable to move
Until the wind comes along
Like objects
With no life in them
A running lady
Late for business
With frizzy orange hair
Bobbing up and down
Like sunflowers
In the wind
A young teenage man
Screwing up his eyes
And looking at his watch
A tall but young girl
Stamping her way
Through crunching leaves
A barking dog
Pulling its owner up a hill
Past decorative lamp posts.

Chloe Nutt (10)
Warren Road Primary School

ANDREW'S DESK

'£2 a peep if you're brave enough,' sang Andrew.
'He ripped me off,' cried Ralph (he was crying).
'Put your ear on my desk and you will hear . . .'
Andrew broke off, Mr Warren-Axe had walked in.
'Sir, if you would care to put your ear against this desk
You are sure to hear good things,' exclaimed Andrew.

Mr Warren-Axe put his ear against the desk.
He heard the scratching of a sharp nail
Scraping down a blackboard,
Then he smelt a foul smelling, rotten egg.

Suddenly Mr Warren-Axe heard a screaming child
That was wailing so loud it hurt his ears.
Then he smelt the scent of a piece of garlic.
A slimy, sticky, hard-boiled sweet was sticking to the desk
'Mr Warren-Axe can I please have my money?'
He left unamused.

As Mr Warren-Axe left, a strange object appeared
Out of the . . .

Phillip Warner (10)
Warren Road Primary School

HAPPINESS

Happiness is the colour of a shining sun,
It tastes like ice cream on a cone.
Happiness is the smell of fresh, green grass,
It looks like the sea brushing backwards and forwards,
It sounds like the chirp of a bird,
It feels like snuggling in a warm bed.

Daniel John Warling (9)
Warren Road Primary School

THE HILLTOP

Overlooking the sunset I stood
Below my feet the raging waves flow
Above my head a starlit sky twinkles
In my pocket a dream come true.

Under the waves a coral reef comes alive
Behind my back a quiet lifeless city sleeps
Over my head several bats fly northwards
In my mind a dream comes true.

In front of me a foggy mist covers the ocean
Behind me a nest of hooting owls flutter
In-between me and the city, a rocky path lies all alone
In my heart a dream comes true.

Rebecca Clark (10)
Warren Road Primary School

ENTERING A CITY

Trees hang over houses
Like long, soft hair
And pass the shadows
Through the blazing light
Angry faces everywhere
For people were bored
Sitting powerless
Adults' faces looking bare
Like trees in winter
Cars move inch by inch
Finally passing through the traffic.

Lucy Royal (10)
Warren Road Primary School

Isabelle's Desk

What's inside Issy's desk?
Maybe a rotten apple
Or some frogs' legs
If you look inside
You may see two eyes.

Pay 5p to look in Issy's desk
One peep and you'll see
An old tomato or a sweet green pea.

They can all hear munching
And a bit of crunching
Like eating a mouldy biscuit.

Issy's desk is terrible
With a sound of lightning
The books rumble on the table.

To everyone's amazement
Out pops a furry leg
And two beady eyes
And . . !

Jessica Corner (10)
Warren Road Primary School

Love

Love is bright pink
And tastes beautifully sweet like soft cream,
Smelling of flowers in a field.
Love looks like a big garden with butterflies flying over flowers.
Love sounds like sweet music being played by a gold flute.
It feels like a comfortable bed with roses over it.

Jessica Barnes (8)
Warren Road Primary School

ENTERING A CITY

The raging faces of drivers
Like those of a wolf
As people make a dash
For the other side
The great glass building
Of a store
Peers down on us
While scowling faces
Load up rubbish
Motorbikes powerless
And trucks stuck
As if glued to the ground.
Shattered shops
Which can't afford repairs
Monstrous cars
Under the power of a simple light
Stuck in traffic
The powerful cars
Overpowered by a pedestrian.

Luke Janes (10)
Warren Road Primary School

SPACE

Every night I look at the stars and think
What the moon looks like in space
And what a black hole looks like from the inside
And how hot the sun is and how it keeps alight
Or how big is a crater
Or what keeps Mars and Pluto in the same place.

James Bowey (9)
Warren Road Primary School

MY CAT

My cat,
Ate a rat,
For tea last night,
She had a fight,
With a big, brown dog.
After the fight
She ate a frog.
My cat came home
With a broken leg,
So we took her to the vet,
She stayed there for seven days,
The dog got told off in all ways.
Finally when my cat came home,
She gave the dog a good beating
With a comb.

Jessica Davis (9)
Weald CP School

MONSTER, MONSTER

Monster, monster! Row, row, row!
Monster, monster! Woe on land!
Monster, monster! Run, run, run!
Monster, monster! Quick in that cave!
Monster, monster! Hide, hide, hide!
Monster, monster! He's coming,
He's coming, he's coming.
Monster, monster! Run! Run!
Run!

Jordan Randall (8)
Weald CP School

I WENT TO SPACE

I went to space
and I cut my face
I felt a disgrace
I wanted to go home
to see my garden gnome.
When I got back
I went to the dome
and buried my face
in colourful foam.
I went to a London ice rink
I felt like I'd gone bright pink
I didn't know why
I looked at the sky
I felt like I was
as fat as a pie.
I went to space
I never came back
because I didn't want
to go through that again.

Oli Priest (9)
Weald CP School

MY OWNER

My owner has a rumply bed
She sometimes doesn't wash.
'Let's play a game,' she sometimes cries
And Teddy you begin
And when we play a game
I wish she'd let me win.

Natasha Rowland (9)
Weald CP School

THE KILLER WHALE

I live by the sea but I have a secret,
I am a mermaid.
I can go on land still.

At night I creep out of the house to the sea,
When I get to the sea, I jump into the sea.
The cool, cool waters touch my skin.

I swim quite a long way out
When I see a movement in the water.
Suddenly I hear a voice, 'A killer whale!'
I see the killer whale coming towards me,
I swim up to him and stroke him.

Suddenly he swims under me
And starts to swim with me on his back.
Beside me a dolphin jumps up
Then a whole herd are jumping beside me.

Then I look down and see a group of turtles,
Then jellyfish all different colours, pink, blue, white.
The killer whale wheels round and heads for the beach,
Then vanishes.
I creep up to the house and slide into bed.
I still dream about the killer whale.

Mary Griffiths (10)
Weald CP School

DWARFS

From over the mountains
To dungeons and caves
For today my dwarfs will find my gold
From the high mountains in the cold.

From ancient kings to elfish lords
To stay today in the blistering hordes
In their huts drinking beer
For me to say today
That dwarfs will live forever.

Mark Minchell (10)
Weald CP School

THE BEACH

I am walking gracefully across the beach,
The sand is hot under my feet.
I lay out my towel on the sand
And listen to the sea playing a band.

I put on my swimming costume
And swim in the sea,
I don't know why people think it's cold,
For it is boiling to me.

I get out of the sea
And dry myself off,
I start to do my homework
'Cause I'm actually a boff!

I put down my pencil
And put down my book,
Take off my towel
And put it on a hook.

I put on my clothes
And leave my feet bare,
I go and look for some shells
For there are shells everywhere.

Emily Kerr (9)
Weald CP School

ALIENS

It was night-time when I saw them,
I saw the UFOs.
They came right into the garden,
As they came out they said their names,
Mars, Venus and the funny thing was
They were all planets,
Jupiter, Moon, Pluto and when they all were out
They looked around and then they went back in backwards
Saying their names backwards,
Sunev, Retipuj, Noom, Otulp,
Then they were gone, back home
And when they had gone out of sight
I heard them say, 'Home sweet home.'

Heather Olley (8)
Weald CP School

CAT

I see a cat laying in the sun
The sun is blazing and I am sweating
Cats are sleeping
Spies peeping
I stroke the cat
Cat yawns
Morning dawns
The cat awakes.

Laura Asplin (8)
Weald CP School

ON THE LINE

Getting warmed up, I'm jogging,
Jumping, I'm stretching my calves
And my hamstrings,
I'm on the line.
On your marks . . . get set . . .
Go.
I'm in the lead, McCarthy has taken over,
I'm back in the lead,
The crowd are cheering,
100 metres to go, 50 metres to go,
5 metres to go,
I'm in the lead . . .
I've won.

Francesca Lee (10)
Weald CP School

MY HAMSTER

My hamster is in his cage,
My hamster is snuggling up in bed,
My hamster is storing his food in his pouch,
My hamster is nearly two,
My hamster is falling asleep,
My hamster is fast asleep,
My hamster is waking up,
My hamster is two,
It's my hamster's birthday,
My hamster is getting old,
My hamster is called Cyril,
But no Cyril anymore,
Why? He is dead.

Nicole Craddock (8)
Weald CP School

MUM

'Mum I don't feel well,
Mum I've got a tummy pain,
Mum I fell,
Mum please tell,
Mum what will I gain?'
'What?'
    'Do
        I
            have
                 to
                     say
                         it
                             again?'

Amy Nicholls (9)
Weald CP School

SHARKS

In the aquarium
Watching the sharks,
Their big yellow teeth
Showing through three inch glass.
The dark black fins
Moving from left to right,
Be careful the glass might break
And the sharks might bite!

Down come the people
To give them fish,
They twirl around them
And take the dish.

Kayla Fourie (9)
Weald CP School